The Management of Counselling and Psychotherapy Agencies

The Management of Counselling and Psychotherapy Agencies

Colin Lago and Duncan Kitchin

SAGE Publications
London • Thousand Oaks • New Delhi

SAGE Publications Ltd
6 Bonhill Street
London EC2A 4PU

SAGE Publications Inc.
2455 Teller Road
Thousand Oaks, California 91320

SAGE Publications India Pvt Ltd
32, M-Block Market
Greater Kailash – I
New Delhi 110 048

British Library Cataloguing in Publication data

A catalogue record for this book is available
from the British Library.

ISBN 0 8039 7994 0
ISBN 0 8039 7995 9 (pbk)

Library of Congress catalog card number 98–61248

Typeset by Photoprint, Torquay, Devon
Printed in Great Britain by Biddles Ltd, Guildford, Surrey

Contents

Foreword

The composition of this book has taken much longer than either our contract with Sage specified or indeed our own expectations forecast. Quite literally, one of us feels he has been 'sleeping on it' for some time, having put the publishers' advance towards a new bed! Rather more seriously, the length of this incubation period has, in part, been determined by the myriad challenges we have been faced with in attempting to address and describe precisely what is required in the management of counselling and psychotherapy agencies.

Almost two decades have now gone by since one of the authors conducted a survey on the establishment of counselling services (Lago, 1981). Many such agencies were then and continue to be, established through the vision, commitment and enthusiasm of their founders (the subject of Chapter 1). The task of management of these organizations has seldom in our experience been considered as of primary importance, certainly in the early years. The vision and commitment have often acted as the binding force for collaboration and productivity. The task of management has, of course, had to be operationalized by various people at various times during these formative stages but our sense is that the need for management in its formal sense has only become fully necessary in the developmental stage following the birth and early infancy of the organization. Before that, enthusiasm and energy will have sufficed to get all the jobs done.

The profession of counselling and psychotherapy has expanded considerably in the last decade of the twentieth century and this development has facilitated the establishment of many more counselling organizations, a wide range of literature, codes of practice and ethics, new training courses and new research. Clients have also become much more sophisticated and knowledgeable of the field and they in their turn (very appropriately), demand the highest standards of professional practice.

These developments will increasingly place demands on organizations offering therapy that they be managed soundly, ethically and professionally. We believe that this book is therefore a timely contribution to those in the profession concerned with the optimum delivery of therapeutic practices. The management of counselling and psychotherapy services should be of concern to all practitioners, not just those appointed as managers. As Carroll and Walton (1997: 1) have so succinctly expressed it:

> understanding that there is more to counselling than what happens in the counselling room enables counsellors to have an eye and perspectives on the 'contexts' in which the counselling takes place.

The overall management task then, in counselling and psychotherapy organizations, is to provide and sustain an optimal context in which therapeutic services may be delivered with sensitivity, care and professionalism.

Despite the assertion above that management should be of concern to all practitioners involved in counselling organizations we are aware that, in practice, a vast number of therapists want little or nothing to do with management, its activities and processes. At its most extreme, this attitude expresses itself in the oversimplistic division between counselling as the pure ethical, uncontaminated expression of honourable intention and management as a tainted and tainting experience full of compromise, domination and Machiavellian intent!

The authors know each other as a result of working at Sheffield University; one as a (now semi-retired) lecturer in management studies who is also trained as a Gestalt therapist and the other who is the Director of the University Counselling Service. Each author has written several chapters, and as a consequence readers may become aware of their different styles. We hope and trust that any dissonance in these styles will not prove overly problematic.

Their cumulative experiences have incorporated working in industry, the youth service, school and higher education, lecturing in management, providing consultancy and staff training to a wide range of statutory, industrial, commercial and voluntary organizations, involvement with counselling and psychotherapy training courses, stress management teaching and working for and on behalf of employee assistance programmes.

Various words have been used interchangeably in the text in order to avoid repetition and/or cause reader boredom and stress! Such word clusters include all those terms that relate to the counselling organization and they include: agency, office, service, institution and organization. Unless specified otherwise in the text, references to colleagues, staff and personnel refer to all the categories of staff employed within a service (eg. receptionists, cleaners, counsellors) whether paid or voluntary. The terms manager and management are used interchangeably in the recognition that a variety of models of management are presently practised including those of the lone manager, job shares and management by committee. We have also used the terms counselling, psychotherapy and therapeutic services interchangeably to maintain both reader interest and consistency with the humanistic (American) literature.

We have attempted, as much as possible, to take into account the management needs of the complete spectrum of counselling and psychotherapy agencies, from impoverished voluntary projects operating a time-limited phoneline service two nights per week to professionally established organizations with full-time staffing complements.

Our initial meetings were consumed by brainstorming ideas, one of which attempted just to list the types of organizations now offering counselling and psychotherapy. This list included the following:

- national phonelines (Childline, HIV helplines)
- counselling/psychotherapy in GP surgeries
- specialist psychotherapy units in the NHS
- school psychological services
- employee assistance programmes
- voluntary organizations (Rape Crisis, Cruse, etc.)
- Relate (and other national bodies)
- women's therapy centres
- youth counselling agencies
- counselling services related to conception, pregnancy, abortions, insemination, etc.
- 'crisis' response teams and organizations (post-traumatic incidents, bank holdups, etc.)

- local phonelines (Samaritans, Gayline, etc.)
- counselling services in schools, further and higher education
- hospice counselling facilities
- counselling psychology/clinical psychology departments
- in-house counsellors (eg. police force counsellors)
- independent psychotherapists and counsellors.

Inevitably there will be many unique aspects to each type of organization depicted above requiring different elements and facets of management.

As a further part of our preparation we interviewed therapists in and read documents from a sizeable sample of the above organization types.

We (bravely!) made attempts to conceptualize these organizational contexts into matrices from which we might deduce particular management requirements or expertise. Similarly, we attempted to explore the different agencies through both (a) an analysis of their resources and (b) an appraisal of their stakeholders. Though profoundly useful in furthering our knowledge of this very wide spectrum of counselling and psychotherapy organizations our attempts to simplify and conceptually synthesize their management requirements into neat packages were, of course, completely frustrated! We hope, nevertheless, that the contents of this book prove useful to those charged with the task of management of counselling agencies.

McLeod (1994b: 163) notes that there has been very little systematic research on the organizational context of counselling. Further, Carroll and Walton (1997: 1) remind us that 'not to recognise and work with the context in which counselling takes place is to ignore the enormous impact that context has on behaviour'. The book attempts to address the very wide range of issues that are involved in the processes of management of therapeutic contexts. Much as the therapist's task is focused on the client, the service manager or management team must concern themselves with optimizing the therapeutic context in which the therapy takes place, having due regard to caring for, supporting and administering the staff team.

The structure of the book starts from the moment of conception of a counselling agency and proceeds to a consideration of the early days of psychotherapeutic services (Chapter 1). Consequently, both Chapters 1 and 2 have titles featuring building metaphors ('laying the foundations' and 'building a sound structure'). Quite literally, the context of any organization necessarily starts with its building and location. Issues related to access, decor, maintenance and so on are thus given appropriate prominence in Chapter 2. Staffing, governance and publicity aspects are also introduced here.

Chapter 3 provides a very focused review of many considerations involved in selecting staff. This is always a complicated arena of management activity and given the increasing number of qualified counsellors and therapists job seeking, combined with the plethora of interview and assessment methods available, managers' headaches can only increase!

In an increasingly litigious climate the themes embodied in Chapter 4 (Ensuring Competent, Professional and Safe Practice) and Chapter 5 (Daily Working Practices) will be of primary and daily importance to those occupying management positions. Add to this responsibility the tasks of Managing Crisis (Chapter 6) and we might hypothesize (in the words of Gilbert) 'that a (manager's) lot is not a happy one!'

The book, to this point, has taken as its focus a wide range of concerns that appropriately and legitimately can be described as management activity. What does the manager have to do, how often, with whom, for whom, how, when, why? Many of these issues are detailed in Chapters 1 to 6.

But what of managing itself? What is managing? How is it done? How does someone train for it? What are the challenges and pitfalls? Chapter 7 attempts to address some of these questions. We were concerned that many therapists might suddenly find themselves in management positions having not really been prepared or trained to fulfil such roles.

Earlier in this introduction we alluded to the perceptual and attitudinal splits that can exist between being a therapist and being a manager. Many counsellors have actively chosen to become so, dedicating themselves to professional and personal development in order to offer optimal therapeutic resources to clients. For some therapists, the interviewing room and the individualized focus of the work offers quiet, secluded refuge in which they aspire to assist their clients plant the necessary seeds of growth.

This very special working atmosphere carries with it the danger, we believe, of becoming an entrapping environment for the therapist. The challenges inherent in management, especially for the promoted therapist could be formidable and not at all desirable. All outside the counselling room is not safe, contained, paced and boundaried! Checking the contents of the first aid box, drawing up staffing schedules, running staff meetings, representing the organization at civic and fund-raising functions, directing colleagues, etc., etc. are considerable challenges. It is our experience that many therapists are now actively not seeking management opportunities precisely because of the perceived demands of the management role. Management, in this sense, may be part of the therapists' shadow world, an element that can be projected upon, ignored, denied, resisted and so on.

This book, however, is for everyone involved in counselling and psychotherapy agencies. Research has indicated how substantive the client's contribution is to the successful outcome of therapy. Similarly, all colleagues involved in counselling organizations have a part to play in the management efforts of those organizations. Teams work much better when pulling together, their final achievements being much more than the sum of their individual parts!

In the words of one author who was involved in the establishment of a counselling service:

> . . . avoid unnecessary committees, keep the organization and language of the venture simple and business like. Don't be seduced by counselling jargon and keep the whole enterprise well spread with humour! (Burrows, 1995: 123)

If only . . . !

Acknowledgements

To my previous management role models, particularly Peter Duke, Arthur Harvey and Jean Clark.

To all the colleagues from whom, under whom and with whom I have learnt about the struggles and joys of management.

To my two long-term clinical supervisors, Dr Bernard Ratigan and David Rose, with whom I have chewed over the organizational cud (crud) more than once!

I am deeply indebted to my parents Owen and Edith for the grounding they gave me in industriousness and fair play, and to my immediate family Gill, Rebecca and James for their love and support.

Finally, I must record a huge thank you to Christine Davison who has committed so many versions of this text to the word processor whilst simultaneously taking care of 15 appointment diaries in our service and all the consequent administration a busy agency demands.

Colin Lago

To Mrs Pollard, the first teacher by whom I felt noticed; Mrs Smith, the first teacher who gave me an inkling that I could be an able student; Caroline Maudling, Ken Evans and Ian Greenway, the therapists who have helped me grow. Without these people I doubt that I would have been in a position to contribute to this book.

Finally, a big thank you to Anneliese who has brought me to life.

Duncan Kitchin

We would both like to thank Colin Feltham and Susan Worsey for their patience and forbearance in the late deliverance of this text and for Colin's extremely helpful editorial comments.

Our thanks also go to many colleagues in different agencies who assisted us in compiling this book.

Colin Lago and Duncan Kitchin

1

Laying the Foundations: Creating a Counselling Service

> A considerable number of Counselling Services have become established in the United Kingdom during the last fifteen years. Inevitably, the establishment of these services has reflected an enormous amount of hard work and planning by the various persons and committees involved. Clearly, the nature and philosophy of these emerging projects will reflect both their individual aims and unique structures as well as their more global drive to provide counselling type resources.
>
> (Lago, 1981)

Almost two decades have now elapsed since the article from which the above quote is taken, was written. In this intervening period considerable expansion has taken place within the world of counselling and this is reflected in a much wider range of services now available. Nevertheless, many would argue that the levels and distribution of counselling provision are still in-adequate, patchy, under-resourced, over-reliant on voluntary con-tribution and effort and under-researched. This general inadequacy of counselling facilities exists in the face of an increasing rise in need, demand and expectations of counselling in society at the present time. Many more counselling services are needed and we hope this book will be helpful to all those involved in such endeavours, as well as to those services already in existence.

Historic Origins

> When people ask 'How did the Counselling Centre begin?' the answer is not the short, simple one they probably expect. It is actually a glimpse into the social history representing the changing face of the caring professions in the twentieth century. (James et al., 1985)

The above quote is taken from an article describing the establishment and structure of the Nottingham Counselling Centre and was made in the context of its historical origins in the Charity Organization Society established in 1875. A diagram of organizational development (similar to a family tree) is provided below (see Figure 1.1). From this diagram one may see the emergence of a range of different organizations, with different emphases geared towards serving the needs of the community and reflecting the ideas and concerns of those particular times.

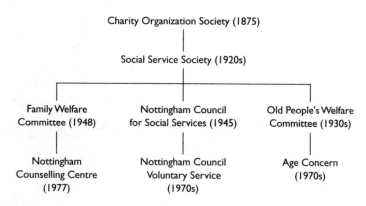

Figure 1.1   *Diagram of Organizational Development (James et al., 1985)*

An overall analysis of the above diagram reveals that the changes of name and directions of the organization have occurred at intervals of between 25 and 40 years. Many of the counselling services referred to in the opening quote of this chapter will now have been in existence for three or more decades and many structural changes will have occurred in the interim. Nevertheless, locating the cornerstones and laying the foundations upon which to build a sound professional structure remains as important today for new organizations as does the ongoing capacity for existing organizations to embody structural changes when required.

Why Counselling? Why Now?

The following slogan was recently featured in an advertisement on behalf of the National Society for the Prevention of Cruelty to Children. 'What she needs is a good listening to.'

Recently, both the Midland Bank and the Labour Party coined the use of the term 'listening' within their slogans and advertising literature. The Labour Party thus became 'the listening party' and the Midland 'the listening bank'. It is suggested here that such advertising terminology was no accident but an attempt to create an ideological perspective based upon trends recognizable as current in society.

Listening, of course, is a central activity in counselling and psychotherapy. So is empathy. As a technical concept that owes much of its origins to the development of the work of Dr Carl Rogers in client-centred therapy, over 20 different definitions have now been developed, including an extensive treatment of it by Rogers himself. Not lagging far behind, marketing personnel have appended the term to a range of beauty products, including that of Empathy shampoo! Similarly, at about the same time, a security company developed the slogan 'Securicor Cares'. Care of others, in the general sense, is embodied within the concept of counselling. 'Care' also is a mnemonic for Rogers' core therapeutic conditions of counselling.

C.A. – communicated authenticity (congruence, genuineness)

R. – regard (acceptance, warmth)

E. – empathy

However interesting, ironic and humorous the above examples may be, they do give an indication of the impact of ideas, derived from counselling and psychotherapy, upon society during the last decades. This is also revealed by a research survey conducted on behalf of the Royal College of Psychiatrists in 1991 that showed that 85 per cent of the 2000 respondents believed that depression was caused by life events and that counselling, not medication, was the most appropriate form of assistance. A decade or two previously, medication was the preferred model.

Helena Kennedy, QC, has recently established a very strong case for increased counselling and psychotherapeutic care of young people who get into trouble (Katz, 1995). Many children who go on to become persistent offenders can apparently be identified at eight to ten years old. The economics of incarceration, of keeping a child in a young offender institution are considerable, indeed more than at the most expensive public schools. Under 16s presently represent 20 per cent of the population and yet expenditure on child and adolescent mental health represents only 5 per cent of the total spent on mental health services.

Both of the above examples are indicative of the belief systems in contemporary society at the present time that see the appropriateness of counselling intervention, despite resistant and persistent policies of non-investment. For example, child psychotherapy is the only NHS-recognized profession for which trainees must fund their own training!

Counselling approaches are generally seen as valid, relevant and effective in this culture at this time (McLeod, 1993). Indeed, Wood (1990) has elaborated further on this theme of 'fit' between therapy and culture, recognizing the importance of cultural acceptability of the healing form. Describing counselling as a 'subtle but powerful ritual' he recognizes that the ritual may be on the cutting edge of cultural change. The relationship, therefore, between a culture and its healing rituals is an interesting and complex one.

McLeod (1993: 8–16) in his book *An Introduction to Counselling* traces the historic and cultural origins of counselling. Citing a range of sources, he asserts that the origins of counselling and psychotherapy as we know them today can be traced back to the beginning of the eighteenth century, which represents a turning point in the social construction of 'madness'. A shift occurred at this time, from dealing with problems encountered in living through religious perspectives implemented at community level towards the 'medicalization' and individualization of human difficulties.

This historic period incorporates the major changes involved in society moving from a predominantly rural/agricultural base to an industrial one. Through the industrial revolution, capitalism began to dominate economic and political life and the values of science began to replace those of religion. In addition, Albee (1977) has argued that this emerging capitalism required the development of a high level of rationality accompanied by repression and control of pleasure seeking. This required the development of a work ethic, an increase in personal autonomy and independence. The accompanying psychological shift that occurred was from a 'tradition-centred' society to one in which inner direction was emphasized. A basis for this shift to secular individualism had already been laid by the philosopher, Descartes, in the seventeenth century (Flew, 1972). Through recognizing the movement from small rural communities where everyone knew everyone else and behaviour was monitored and controlled by others, to urban industrial societies where life was much more anonymous and internally focused, one may understand some of the underlying historical conditions that have led to contemporary forms of interpersonal help, which focus on the individual, inner life of the person.

Prior to the eighteenth century, people who suffered mental ill health would have been nursed by their extended families and local communities. The advent of larger urban areas, factory conditions, fragmentation of communities and greater anonymity between people eventually led to the establishment of workhouses and asylums – society-based responses. People who were deemed mad or insane were certainly not productive and in many cases were disruptive. It is not appropriate here to provide a wealth of detail of this period, interesting though it is, but it is crucial to understand that through this historical period the medical profession came to assume control over asylums (Scull, 1975). The defeat of moral treatment can be seen as a key moment in the history of psychotherapy: science replaced religion as a dominant ideology underlying the treatment of the insane (McLeod, 1993).

New medical–biological explanations for insanity were formulated and many different types of physical treatment were experimented with (Scull, 1979). By the end of the nineteenth century psychiatry had achieved a dominant position in the care of the insane. According to Ellenberger (1970) the earliest physicians to call themselves psychotherapists were Van Renterghem and Van Eeden who opened a clinic of suggestive psychotherapy in

Amsterdam in 1887. Thus, the first clinic for suggestive psychotherapy was established one century ago. Many more 'clinics' have
only recently formed and we trust that some of the cumulative
learnings gained during this historical process will inform this
book.

A Rationale for Creating a New Counselling Service

Meeting the Need

> In the beginning it is helpful to establish whether there is a real need
> . . . (BAC Information Sheet 12)

A preliminary survey carried out by Lago (1981) on the establishment of counselling projects provided a range of data on the
background and origin of some counselling organizations. In
response to one question on the survey, asking 'What needs did
you seek to meet?', a very wide range of responses were received.
Approximately one-third of the respondents cited quite wide
definitions, eg. 'to help young people in distress', 'to help people
facing problems of life, faith and relationships', 'to meet the needs
of the lonely and depressed', 'to provide a friendly ear to troubled
persons'. In this survey 33 replies were received and a third of
these provided very clear responses in relation to the specific
client group of young people. Items such as homelessness, drugs,
unemployment, pregnancy and psycho-sexual counselling were
listed.

Other reasons given seemed to focus on filling gaps of provision
in the existing range of local authority services and voluntary
organizations. One such example that we encountered whilst
collecting data for this book was that of a women's counselling
centre that had come into being mainly out of the recognition
of a specific set of needs not being met by any other local
organization.

At least two of the organizations we consulted indicated that
the motivating forces behind their establishment were to do with
a juxtaposition of two elements: (i) a hunch/hypothesis that such
a need existed and (ii) the enthusiasm, commitment and readiness
of the original founders to create such an organization. This
dedication, vision and enthusiasm of founding figures (described
in 1995 as heroes and heroines by John McLeod in a private

telephone conversation on the subject of this book) seems to form an additional aspect required to complete the full equation, ie. perceived need of a client group + the human therapeutic capacity to respond (heroes & heroines) = foundation stones of counselling service. We will return to this aspect a little later in the chapter.

Evidence of Need

Evidence of need quoted in the early survey by Lago spanned the complete spectrum from personal hunch and intuition through to statements citing fieldwork evidence, surveys and research (Lago, 1981: 21). Fieldwork evidence formed the basis of two-thirds of the survey responses. Within this category, the impression created was that of a wide range of working experiences being gained by different people occupying various roles within a community who had begun to ask the questions 'what is happening here?', 'where could these people be referred?', 'how come there is no organization to respond to such important needs?', and so on.

Only three projects were based on existing research and survey results. Three further projects opted to initiate an experimental trial run of the counselling service in order to test the extent of local needs.

A recent example of this last category was that of a GP surgery which had initially contracted in a counsellor to facilitate a staff group comprising nurses and doctors. This introductory phase enabled the staff at the surgery to become more fluent with and understanding of the work of counsellors. This first experience, which was a positive one, developed into offering part-time employment to the counsellor within the surgery. Starting at 5 hours per week, and paid for through ancillary staffing budgets, this commitment eventually grew to almost full-time with a constant waiting list of patients needing to be seen.

Predating most of the above projects, the National Marriage Guidance Council came into being in the late 1930s and early 1940s. During the previous two decades there had been extensive public debate over the nature of marriage. Lewis et al. (1992) describe this era as one in which marriage began to change from being a public social institution to becoming more of a private interpersonal relationship. One of the visible signs of these funda- mental social changes was the increased frequency of divorce. McLeod (1994b) records that in response to these social and cultural forces, it was argued that something needed to be done to support marriage.

One important aspect of evidence of need is demonstrated with this example above. That is, there had begun to exist a state of 'social awareness' in relation to changes that were happening to the institution of marriage. Further evidence of ongoing need was provided by the London office (of Marriage Guidance), who were receiving, by the autumn of 1945, 4000 letters per month seeking help (Wallis and Booker, 1958). This particular example of one of the most well-known counselling organizations in Britain, is a powerful model demonstrating fit between societal trends and the responses of individuals and organizations committed to meeting specific needs.

Most recent examples of this 'society–organization fit' include the considerable spread of counselling availability within General Practice surgeries and the increase in employee assistance programmes available to the employees of large companies.

'Visionaries, Heroes and Heroines'

In a telephone conversation with one of the authors, John McLeod acknowledged that having spent some considerable time researching his article on 'issues in the organization of counselling' he had come to be interested in the conceptual work of the organizational theorists, Hasenfeld and Schmid, in the role of the early instigators of counselling organizations. These, he termed 'visionaries, heroes and heroines'.

Hasenfeld and Schmid (1989) suggest the existence of six stages within the life-cycle of a social service organization: formation, collectivity, formalization, elaboration of structure, decline and death.

Stage one they describe as the formation/entrepreneurial stage. The key features of this stage are described as the organization existing within an unstable, unknown external environment where there is uncertainty over resources, the organization is small with an informal structure and management style and is seeking a market for its services. Our various researches for this book, gained both through articles and lengthy discussions with organizations, revealed many references to the work of their early pioneers and founders (Burrows, 1995; The Group at the Francis Centre, 1984; Lago, 1981; Wallis and Booker, 1958). They are variously described as follows:

In 1980, four people met together with the intention of setting up a counselling centre in Derby. They were a Methodist Minister, the wife of a dispensing chemist, a Canon of the Cathedral and a re-evaluation counselling resource person who was also a liberal studies lecturer and human relations trainer. These were soon joined by an ex-Probation Officer who was interested in the fields of bio feedback and bio-energetics. (The Group at the Francis Centre, 1984)

The original proposal to set up a counselling service came from two far-seeing ministers . . . (Burrows, 1995)

The research carried out for these papers was initiated by a request to myself from Michael Jacobs, the counsellor at the University of Leicester who had earlier formally approached the British Association for Counselling to seek its help and support in the possible formation of a counselling service in Leicester. (Lago, 1981)

My own memory of that time is that having just completed my training I knew I neither wished to work on my own nor within a large organization. In conversations with Brian (Thorne) and later with Michael (Da Costa) we came to feel that there was a potential role for a counselling centre within and for the city. Faith (Broadbent) and Aude (De Souza) also soon joined us to facilitate the movement of this vision into a reality. (Conradi, 1995)

The six-stage model of organizational development previously mentioned carries with it, by inference, a demand upon the necessary skills and aptitudes available to the managers and other personnel appropriate to each stage of the development process. The pioneers of counselling organizations necessarily must have (and if more than one, be united in their) vision, tenacity, stamina, a capacity to excite and involve others and an ability to articulate the vision to a wide range of people in the community. Other personal attributes would include the capacities to withstand and tolerate anxiety and pressure of demand, to embody hope, to empower and to stimulate.

Inevitably, the majority of visionaries, heroes and heroines revealed by Lago's survey (1981) comprised people who were in the main already engaged in the caring professions, eg. social workers, probation officers, youth workers, priests and counsellors. Almost two decades later, following considerable developments in the profession of counselling and psychotherapy that have been closely parallelled by society's awareness levels of such facilities, it is hypothesized that, today, the pioneers of new services will, mostly, already be fully qualified psychotherapeutic professionals (eg. counsellors, psychotherapists, counselling psychologists) (see, for example, Carsley, 1995). Lay professionals are much less likely to be involved than they were historically.

Stakeholder Analysis

The preceding sections have provided a brief historical overview of the relationship between some changing aspects of society and counselling organizational responses to such need. The literature quoted earlier has given a snapshot of the early visions and determination, often by non-qualified counsellors, to establish appropriate and relevant counselling facilities capable of addressing specific and various social needs. The voluntary sector within British society has a long and noble history distinguished by the provision of timely and radical services devised to meet and respond to new social difficulties. Counselling organizations have, in the last 20 years, become part of that noble historic development.

Given the contemporary awareness of counselling as a helping process, however, we contend that the use of a simplified model of stakeholder analysis might prove one very useful way of laying the foundations. In essence, a stakeholder analysis offers a method of identifying the principal players (those that have a stake) in any given situation. We have transformed this idea into a series of questions which potential pioneers and visionaries might usefully address.

- How is the evidence of need assessed (for a counselling service)?
- Who wants a counselling service?
- Who is driving the need? (The potential clients, counsellors or an overall organization eg. a hospital or a major employer, etc.)
- To what extent might clients be involved in the organization?

Answers to the above might then lead on to the following questions of organizational design and structure.

- What sort of organization would be most appropriate to meet the need? (eg. an in-house service or one commissioned from outside, a telephone service or one that provides face-to-face counselling)
- What is the scale of service envisaged?

- What methods might be used for estimating possible service usage?
- What other evidence of need is there?

All the above questions are likely to be relevant to anyone contemplating the creation of a counselling service. As such, they are probably as useful to a group of enthusiastic members of a community centre wishing to do something useful for local people as a large multinational organization wanting a counselling service for its employees. Two decades ago, however, examples of large commissioning organizations hardly existed. Nowadays they are more prevalent and, consistent with the trends of counselling sophistication in society, are often extremely well informed of why they want a counselling service and what they want from it.

Contemporary pioneers then, who are intent on creating an organization, for example, whose services can be contracted in, will necessarily have to be extremely well informed and established with very professional operating structures and conditions, and have a high quality of professional presentation. They would require:

- clear statements of codes of ethics and practice
- clear definitions of precise services offered
- evidence of supplementary and back-up facilities including psychiatric and medical care, insurance arrangements
- complaints procedures
- evidence of professional qualifications/suitability of their counsellors
- provision of and articulated necessity for supervision
- evidence of monitoring practices
- provision of sound and discrete interviewing facilities
- provision of clear mechanisms for referrals and appointments
- published availability of counsellors/service (eg. 24 hours, on call or 9am.–5pm. weekdays)
- provision of information feedback loops (or not) to contracting organization
- reference to individual and organizational membership of appropriate professional bodies and so on
- equal opportunities statements
- evaluation procedures.

Summing Up

The impact of social history upon counselling provision is well evidenced in this chapter. As society's awareness and acceptance of counselling and psychotherapy have developed, so too have organizations evolved in their services and professional bodies have expanded in membership, service provision and indeed professional authority. This social phenomenon of development and change between need and response, between individual and society, is a sociologically complex one but one that requires the attention of any 'visionaries' wishing to establish a counselling service. Two decades of change in the late twentieth century have dramatically altered the constituent elements that are now required in the creation of new services.

2

Building a Sound Structure: Management Issues

> Staff felt very strongly that the new Counselling Centre must be based on firm foundations with clear aims and working procedures.
>
> (James et al., 1985)

The preceding chapter, in addition to addressing the social and historical context within which counselling has developed during the last half century also referred to the processes of organizational change over time (Hasenfeld and Schmid, 1989). 'Building a sound structure', the title of this chapter, implies a 'once and for all' set of building tasks, which, when in place, remain for ever (or at least a considerable amount of time). By contrast, and in reality, the task of management is a continuous one constantly monitoring, adjusting and 'oiling' the organization. Our apologies are due here for mixing two metaphors above, that of (i) a fixed structure, eg. a building and (ii) a machine with many moving and interconnecting parts.

Both metaphors apply simultaneously in management, ie. sufficient 'bricks' (building, systems, policies, procedures) need to be in place to provide a secure infrastructure for the organization and sufficient 'oiling' (enabling, responding, requesting, directing, overseeing) has to be constantly provided to respond to the ever changing, fluid situation within the organization. Further, the demands of managing will be heightened, from time to time, because of particular events or crises and/or in relation to the overall development of the organization over time. Using the conceptual system developed by Hasenfeld and Schmid (1989) one may see how different demands on management are made by changes in organizational structure, size, usage and overall development of the unit.

This chapter now considers some of the particular issues and aspects subsumed under the two categories above, that of structure and that of process.

Primary Structures – the Location and Premises

> Quiet, pleasant, informal rooms are essential, free of busy noticeboards with ease of access and where confidentiality will be respected. (BAC Information Sheet 12)

Needless to say, the practicalities associated with the 'bricks and mortar', the building where the agency conducts its work, are considerably determined by an enormous range of issues. From a manager's perspective, the building might be a received given, and very little may be able to be done with this 'fact'. The agency may have been donated the building by a charity or leased the premises by a local authority. It might have been directed to the location by a large employer (eg. a student counselling service within a university) or received the building in bequest. All of the above circumstances coalesce into a particular 'given' for the management whose task will then be to ensure the optimization of the facilities for the specific purposes of the counselling agency.

Possibilities of choice of location do occur at particular stages of an organization's development (eg. at the outset or when the agency outgrows its premises through increased usage) or at moments of crisis, incurred for example when buildings might be repossessed or condemned and are thus withdrawn from the agency's use. Where choice exists, those directly concerned with the management of the agency have to consider a complex range of facts. In an extended consideration of these issues, Lago and Thompson (1996: Chapter 9) discussed the following major themes: location of the counselling agency; access routes/

signposting, etc.; and appropriateness of internal decor and style.

Temenos

The Greek term *temenos* was originally ascribed as a sacred field, 'my father's park and fruitful vineyard' (from Homer, 1919, quoted in Embleton Tudor and Tudor, 1995). The Tudors also quote two definitions for the term taken from Liddell and Scott (1901): (i) A piece of land cut or marked off, assigned as an official domain; (ii) A piece of land marked off from common uses and dedicated to a god. These definitions related the concept to both the material and spiritual worlds. Somewhat parallel concepts can be found both in the Indian and Islamic traditions (Embleton Tudor and Tudor, 1995: 2). Wittgenstein and Jung both contributed to the more recent understandings of this term (Embleton Tudor and Tudor, 1995: 2/3).

In short, the value of *temenos* here is in stimulating counsellors to reflect seriously on the nature of the therapeutic space they provide for clients. This space will extend physically all the way from the boundary fence and garden gate (depicted in Figure 2.1) to the interviewing room via reception, with concomitant psychological effects for both clients and counselling agency staff.

Edward Hall (1969), the anthropologist, has written extensively on space and context within the transcultural field. Some cultures deliberately provide public buildings that are socially conducive and relevant to the proceedings that take place within them. In addition, Hall also draws our attention to the fact that some cultures, more than others, place a sense of meaning upon the context of a particular meeting rather than, for example, upon the verbal utterances or conversations that take place within it (Hall, 1983).

Arising from the above, various questions can be elicited to aid the considerations surrounding the optimization of an agency's location and these are considered below.

Location and Access

These have to be considered in relation to ensuring ease of access by the potential client population. How will clients travel to the agency? How will they find the agency? How will it be signposted or advertised?

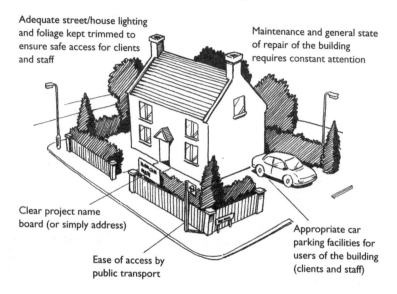

Adequate street/house lighting and foliage kept trimmed to ensure safe access for clients and staff

Maintenance and general state of repair of the building requires constant attention

Clear project name board (or simply address)

Ease of access by public transport

Appropriate car parking facilities for users of the building (clients and staff)

Figure 2.1 *Issues in the Location of and Access to an Organization Offering Therapy*

Initial responsibility for the appropriate provision of therapeutic surroundings rests primarily within the management function. The term 'management function' here is used within its widest context, as the authors know of very different examples of management structures overseeing the development of buildings and rooms on behalf of counselling agencies. These working examples span the spectrum of: (i) individual managers conducting all negotiations and making all arrangements themselves; and (ii) management committees working on behalf of the counselling team. In other examples the counsellors themselves, working as a co-operative, not only have made all the decisions but also have decorated and furnished the facilities.

Location, access and decor are all interrelated themes within the client's experiential frame and as such deserve considerable thought. Not all factors, of course, can be controlled or the complete range of client perceptions be anticipated or indeed known. Nevertheless, an overall 'management' perspective is required on the physical process of access to the agency, from the street to the front door and then from reception to the waiting room and finally the counselling room, as these elements will all have an impact upon the client. A worthwhile experiment to carry out at this stage would be to walk through or be wheeled through (anticipating the case of wheelchair-bound clients) this sequence of stages both during the daytime and evening time during winter months, taking note of one's reactions in the process. Appropriate refinements may then be conducted in the light of the results obtained.

Maintenance, Cleaning and Overall Safety
Leading on directly from the above, responsibility for repairs, bulb replacements, keeping access routes clear and so on must be within someone's job specification. Safety regulations, fittings, equipment and procedures will also require enormous attention at the outset of moving into a new building and then a monitoring 'eye' will need to be maintained throughout usage.

Safety aspects will include:

- general condition of building
- regular and prompt repairs to damages
- regular cleaning
- clear access/exit routes
- signed access/exit routes
- fire safety aspects (provision of extinguishers, fire doors, fire escapes, fire blankets, smoke alarms)
- security alarm (fitting and maintenance)
- building security (who locks up, what is locked up, security lighting, etc.)
- thermal control (what form of heating, maintenance, safety of portable heaters, fans, etc.)
- even floor coverings (loose carpet on stairways can be very dangerous)
- electrics (wiring, fuse boxes, etc.).

The list above not only depicts the importance of a range of duties that require regular completion through assigned responsibilities to particular staff but also includes the wider implications of staff training in relation to safety and administration systems to complete in relation to 'incidents'. Emergency episodes or crisis incidents have the frightening potential to expose gaps in thought, procedures and provision in organizations. During the writing of this book the authors heard about quite a wide range of such examples. These included a staff member seriously damaging a hip when falling on an ice covered path that gave access to the agency, a client having a fit whilst in counselling, a client coming for interview in a seriously overdosed state necessitating yet refusing hospitalization and the fire alarm going off during a peak interviewing time.

The potentially wide range of incidents that could occur can have the effect of inducing some considerable anxiety in managers! However, the implementation of some mechanisms and strategies might not only provide reassurance to the manager but more importantly equip the agency to manage such incidents with the maximum of safety, efficiency and limited disturbance to others in the building (not possible, of course, in the incidence of fire where all occupants must leave on the alarm sounding). Such mechanisms should include:

- staff training and awareness in relation to first aid and fire regulations
- provision of first-aid facilities and persons competent in first aid
- maintenance of an incidents reporting procedure (forms, book, file, etc.).

Decor, Room Usage and Safety

It is reasonable to meet the person in the reception area and show them to the counselling room. It is best if the room is reasonably airy, warm and uncluttered, with comfortable chairs. A box of tissues is usually considered essential! Take all reasonable precautions to ensure that you are not distracted once the session commences; disconnect telephones, ensure nobody will knock at your door and make certain you are not required to answer intercom systems. The room will hopefully be well insulated acoustically to prevent sound entering or leaving, particularly if it adjoins a reception area. With growing concerns over physical violence, books considering the issues surrounding violence and offering practical guidance have emerged. (Breakwell, 1989 quoted in Ruddell, 1997: 17).

The quote used above also refers to growing concerns expressed by health care professionals over physical violence. Every care must be taken to ensure that sufficient mechanisms are put in place that could be mobilized at times of emergency. These might include: the installation of a panic button or emergency alarm in each interviewing room; policies on interviewing that ensure that this never occurs if the building is otherwise empty; and alerting other colleagues to the possibility of violence and asking that they keep an ear open.

The therapeutic aspects of space and surroundings introduced in the earlier section on *temenos* are rendered most explicit by the choice of wallpaper, furniture, visual images, objets d'art, curtain materials and so on. Interior designers, of course, make a living from conceptualizing interiors and creating particular 'ambiences' or atmospheres within domestic and public buildings. Our intention here, which is without aspirations or pretensions towards a counselling agency hiring such professionals, is, nevertheless, to encourage very conscious reflection and planning where decor and furnishings are involved. The creation of therapeutic space deserves and demands more than the idle 'throwing together' of odd bits of furniture and old rugs. However impoverished the agency is, creative colleagues have a tremendous capacity to make the most of quite minimal resources.

Often overlooked is the question of the kind of therapeutic activity envisaged within the agency, eg. primal/Gestalt/psychodramatic work may necessitate extra soundproofing, floor cushions, punchbags, etc. and group work/couple work may simply require more space. Aside from the visual aspects of the environment (colours, fabrics, pictures, etc.) heat, light and smell will also be important to attend to. Very cold buildings and rooms do not encourage self-revelation and enquiry! Low levels of light can encourage deep revelations according to Carsley (1995) but might create apprehension in the early stages. Smells also will affect the ambience. Some therapists value open windows or burn oils or joss sticks to create an ambience.

Harnessing the good will and talents of agency colleagues in this venture of decor and furnishing is not only a management function but can provide a wonderful basis for team building. Once a counselling organization is up and running, very few opportunities exist other than staff meetings and occasional training seminars where staff can work alongside one another so creatively and co-operatively.

Staffing Structures

The counselling work and management of LCP will be interrelated. It will be necessary for a system of decision making and accountability to be established. A General Assembly of all those involved in LCP is proposed. It will be a gathering where workers can talk to each other, give and receive support and criticism and where policy is made and changed. It may be necessary for a small executive group to emerge out of the assembly and for individuals to be selected to co-ordinate aspects of the work. (Ratigan, 1981)

At the time of writing the above piece, the Leicester Counselling Project (LCP) was embarking on a very important series of developmental steps towards becoming an established counselling centre. The idea of a general assembly of all those involved was in fact a continuation of the early public meetings called by Michael Jacobs and colleagues to stimulate the formation of the LCP.

The term 'staffing structure', used above to introduce this section, is intended as a descriptive term to apply to any conceptual system that depicts a set of purposeful working relations between the various personnel engaged in the agency. There are several ways in which managers might construct such 'pictures' of their organizations. These may include:

(a)   diagrams of role authority and responsibility in the organization
(b)   job specifications for individuals
(c)   defined uses of group and committee structures and how these complement the daily working practices
(d)   task specifications for particular groups (eg. advertising, security, finance)
(e)   'sub-group' diagrams. These might be helpful, for example, in circumstances where a team of part-time counsellors is employed. (The 'Tuesday' shift might seldom meet the 'Wednesday' shift for example and so systems for cross-shift communication need to be devised.) The 'Tuesday' shift for example might have a quite different role profile to other shifts. It may be charged with different types of work, have a different management person, have different reception arrangements to the other shifts and so on. Where these systems are sufficiently different or unique compared with the overall system, a 'sub-group' diagram or description may be most useful.

How people are brought together to maximize their involvement and potential within an organizational structure is a considerable challenge to those charged with management responsibilities. Various writers concerned about the organization of counselling highlight the distinctions and tensions inherent between the inner and the outer, counselling work and administration, responsibility to clients and accountability to governing bodies, psychotherapeutic processes and the mores of society (Burrows, 1995; McLeod, 1994a, b). These tensions, at worst, have the potential to completely sabotage the work of an organization. Counsellors and administrators may begin to assume 'sides' and unhelpful projections become consolidated within the staff team, thus hindering working relationships. At worst, this ferment of tension can impact upon others outside the immediate organization, eg. supervisors, other agencies, referral agents, etc. Consequently, the management task in the first instance is to create a sufficiently clear, coherent and workable structure for the agency workforce. In addition, this structure needs to be simple enough to be readily accessible to understanding by all involved and to be seen by the staff as a helpful mechanism that will further enhance the agency's work through collaborative and co-operative endeavour.

Many factors will, of course, influence the structure's design. These will include:

■ number of personnel involved
■ nature of employment contracts (part-time, full-time, voluntary, etc.)
■ nature of different role functions to be performed (counsellors, receptionists, cleaners, security, managers, finance officer, etc.)
■ lines of responsibility
■ lines of communication
■ other mechanisms to ensure maximum communication (staff meetings, newsletters, etc.)
■ relationship of organization to funding bodies
■ relationship of organization to the context within which it is involved (eg. an employee assistance scheme contracted to a large employer, a counselling service within an NHS facility).

A strong assumption underpins this complete section. That is, that the organization is geared and motivated to achieve the maximum and most effective delivery of its services to the client group. For many counselling organizations, notwithstanding the organizational, clinical and other practical difficulties, this may prove a relatively contained task. Their agreed task and modus operandi is to offer counselling only, to individual clients. A simple commercial analogy might be made here of a retail outlet specializing in selling one product only to a limited group of customers. The limited and defined nature of this service delivery offers the management a conceptually simpler task in establishing a nominal structure for all personnel involved. The words 'simple', 'limited' and 'defined' might seem absolutely inappropriate to those experienced in management. Such concepts do not even acknowledge the sheer complexity of managing teams of staff having different personalities, occupying different roles, having differing views of the organization and so on. Nevertheless, a delivery of a singular service to a defined population is conceptually, at the outset, not too challenging.

On the other hand, greater challenge is involved if the organization has a range of services to deliver to a wider population. For example, some employee assistance schemes offer counselling, stress management training, advice to executives, 24-hour telephone lines, various booklets, diagnostic services and so on. These differing services may also be offered to a wider range of clients coming from different organizational settings, referred by self, colleagues or senior staff for particular reasons or services. The referrers themselves might also expect a particular service from the counselling agency. This increasingly complex scenario introduces a new range of working complexities and subtleties that will have to be conceptualized and fitted into the staffing structure in order that the various demands are met and dealt with professionally, legally, ethically and financially. A tall order indeed!

An apology has already been given above for the suggestion that the construction of a system of staffing functions and relationships is potentially a simple task. The application of any system on to people carries with it inherent difficulties of 'person–system' fit. Often, considerable processes of negotiation, taking up much time, are required to ensure that a 'fully adapted' understanding and spirit of co-operation exists between all staff members.

Inevitably, as time proceeds and the counselling agency experiences different changes and challenges, the operating systems will require modification and 'tweaking'. The personnel involved in the system will change over time. Particular relationship difficulties may develop between certain colleagues. Ideological or procedural differences may develop between shifts or sub-groups. All these examples and more will cause great headaches for those charged with the management function. At different times, the manager will have to attend either to the needs of the system or to the personal needs expressed by particular personnel. This tension of managerial duty between systems and personality, between service delivery and disruptive group dynamics, between philosophical ideals and everyday experiencing, is precisely the arena in which the managers may wish for all the wisdom of Solomon and yet feel singularly unable to resolve satisfactorily the predicaments presented.

Managers might benefit greatly from opportunities to have their own supervisor, or management mentor, in order to contemplate and clarify their own position and decisions. The manager has to attend to overall optimization of the service delivery and must also provide some appropriate elements of caring for the staff.

Facilitating and Evaluating the Client's Process through the Agency

Though the following issues are considered in more detail elsewhere in this book, it seems appropriate to refer to them here as aspects of the agency's work that will interact with and be affected by the staff structures discussed previously.

What processes are envisaged for a client from their first point of contact with the service to their eventually being helped and subsequently completing their contract? Such a process requires working procedures in terms of reception of initial contact, proceeding to intake and possible assessment interviews, followed by counselling arrangements and so on. Reception, assessment and counselling staff are already involved in the above scenario and their efforts must be efficiently linked together through both agency policies as well as procedural systems. Absolute care has to be paid to the linking processes between the various personnel denoted in this system in order that the client's overall experience of the process is seen as helpful.

What systems exist for negotiation of payment of fees? Who negotiates? Who decides on difficult cases? Who collects the fees, issues receipts, etc.? Who banks the money and looks after the accounts? Are counselling contracts time-limited or open-ended? What forms of supervision are available to counsellors? Are there sufficient opportunities for case meetings between counsellors themselves and between counsellors, receptionists and supervisors?

The clients' perceptions of and experiences in the agency may also be gathered to assess the efficacy of the overall delivery of the therapeutic experience. Researching the client view is an important element in monitoring the efficacy of the service delivered. Individual clients obviously will not, in most cases, distinguish between their experiences of the people in the agency and the policies and procedures that those people have used. Client feedback might be more generalized into overall perceptions of the agency or the individual counsellor. Therefore, analysing accurately the client feedback will be an important management function, thus equipping the manager with information that may be applied to the system to rectify any shortfalls in delivery.

Going Public: Promotion and Advertising

> I never read a patent medicine advertisement without being impelled to the conclusion that I am suffering from a particular disease therein dealt with in its most virulent form. (Jerome K. Jerome quoted in *Penguin Dictionary of Modern Quotations*, 1976: 115)

The various counselling agencies and organizations we consulted in preparing this text all acknowledged the profound difficulty they experienced in feeling that they had got their advertising 'right'. Of course, this subjective sense of not performing this task well is profoundly understandable when one considers that many of the attributes and characteristics of advertising and public relations are antithetical to those of counselling and psychotherapy. The former activity (advertising) is geared towards a reductionist, sometimes 'snap-shot' description of what is on offer and is presented to the outside world through a range of media; and the latter (counselling and psychotherapy) offers an in-depth, expansionist, intimate exploration of concerns with one other person sealed off in quietness (in a room) and silence (confidentiality as the operating ethic).

The simple lesson that seems to emerge from this is that counsellors are ill equipped to become advertisers and vice versa! However, this is too simplistic a view to sustain with any conviction, as the following story indicates.

One of the authors previously worked for a decade in what was a former polytechnic. The student counselling service there enjoyed good relations with many academic departments including one dedicated to training students in graphics, commercial art and advertising. At different times during this period, the counselling service asked if the graphics students would take on a project of conceptualizing poster advertising for the service. Consultancy meetings would then be held to inform the advertising team about the nature and intention of the work of the counselling service. In the due course of time students would return to present their work. Often, an extraordinarily wide range of images, ideas and slogans had been generated. Many, unfortunately for the designers, could not be used by the counselling service. Graphic cartoon figures wearing prison uniforms trailing a ball and chain behind them with various problem areas depicted inside the ball were considered to be too dramatic in their representation. Other ideas, for a variety of reasons, were also not considered to be acceptable. And occasionally some ideas leapt off the page as really catching a tone or value that the counsellors felt strongly they could identify with.

In the above example, this particular counselling service was most fortunate in being able to access a wide range of expertise freely and having such a wide range of choice of ideas and images from which they could choose particular items. This scenario probably differs very little from the commercial sector. The advertising process is constituted by a partnership between the commissioning industry and the advertising department or agency. The advertisers, after consulting the industry, produce a range of ideas, that are then considered and decided upon by the commissioning industry.

Transposed into the field of counselling, the expertise of the counselling agency will figure primarily in being able to communicate accurately enough what it is they feel it is worth advertising and then latterly in deciding the most appropriate image and style of a possible range that has been proffered. That is, if they are fortunate enough to have an agency produce the advertising.

The introductory paragraphs to this section above have depicted a scenario that has featured notice board advertising only and a relationship with advertising expertise. The latter, for economic reasons, may never be a possibility for many organizations. And suffice it to say, notice board advertising is but one of a wide range of methods for going public and disseminating information about what the agency does.

Different Counselling Organizations, Different
Advertising Needs

The term 'advertising' used in the title above is used with its widest range of honourable meanings intended. The following meanings are contained in the *Concise Oxford Dictionary (1974)*: (a) Advert. Refer to (in speaking or writing); (b) Advertise. Notify, warn, inform . . . make generally known; (c) Advertisement. Public announcement (usually by placards or in journals). *Roget's Thesaurus* also quotes derivations of publicity as publicness and common knowledge (1972: 202).

Advertising in the above senses is thus geared to informing the public via speaking, writing and transmission of images of important information about the organization.

The specific nature of what it is that requires advertising will also change over time. At the outset of an organization, very clear primary information will need to be disseminated to appropriate outlets and potential referring agents in the field. This information may differ depending on who it is targeted towards. If transmitted to professional organizations who may be seen to be the likely sources of referral, the emphasis of the talk or literature will necessarily be focused differently to direct communications with the prospective client population.

Occasional comments made by clients over the years have also alerted the writers to the importance of how and what is advertised and perhaps also reflect the uniqueness of views that different people experience in receiving advertising: '[M]y mum thought I should come and see you because you all looked very friendly in the photograph displayed on your brochure . . .'; 'I remember your organization being referred to several years ago in a lecture . . . and I thought I'd never have to use it then . . .'

The best forms of advertising have the potential to inform accurately and thus act as a form of acculturation or induction for the client. To dare to commit oneself, through making an appointment with a strange or unknown organization, to discussing and confronting one's own worries and difficulties, takes great courage. It is so important that every opportunity should be taken by the agency to help to describe, with accuracy, what might happen, what is the counselling process, how the person will be treated, how soon an appointment might be made, if there is an assessment process, if fees are charged and so on.

Not only is it morally and ethically right to provide accurate information, it is also psychologically right for potential users. From the very first mention of your organization to subsequent descriptions, hearsay, first point of contact and so on, impressions and expectations are being formed of what to expect, what will happen and will it help?

David Brandon quotes from an original Zen story when he refers to the prospective client (and this also will apply to any discerning and caring referral agent) as feeling something like the following: 'If I let you caress my wings, however gently, will I be able to fly again?' (Brandon, nd).

Before even approaching the agency, the client will need to feel secure enough in their faith that the agency is a competent organization that will do its utmost to assist their particular predicament. Publicly available information has an enormous role to play in preparing the client for the experience.

All of the above might be generally applied to a whole range of organizations providing counselling. Particular organizations will, of course, have to focus their advertising carefully because of the nature of their client group, the organization's position relative to wider organizational or community settings, the nature of funding sources and so on. Pictorial images on the advertising will need to be chosen with great sensitivity to the potential client group. Also, counselling agencies that service multiracial areas might need their advertising to be printed in the relevant community languages. (This latter point has to be considered carefully in relation to the agency's capacity to offer counselling in those languages.)

A counselling facility offered within a GP surgery has no need to advertise publicly. Nevertheless, the referring agents (eg. the doctors or practice manager) will need to be advised of the counsellor's work and possibly trained in good referral skills in relation to their patients.

One women's therapy service we consulted employed a variety of methods to advertise its inception including talks to groups of professionals (nurses, doctors, social workers); general information to libraries, doctors' surgeries, community centres, city information centres; and more specific information to women's groups and organizations on its specialist services (eg. eating disorders, sexual abuse). One rural counselling service also used local newspapers and displayed advertising in market places, farming newsletters, café notice boards and church halls.

*Other Advertising Activities and the Importance of
Naming*

One last example is of a counselling centre that wished to make
itself available to anyone in the city and its environs. In addition to
employing some of the above advertising ideas it also ran various
training group and educational events at weekends and on mid-
week evenings. The existence and tenor of the organization could
thus be appropriately disseminated through its other professional
activities. Indeed, the founding group of this particular centre was
very concerned to establish an organization that would emanate
and be associated with professional and humane values and
consequently spent some considerable time deciding upon an
appropriate agency name. The name of the organization might
prove the very fountainhead from which all other information and
advertising will flow.

What is in a name? Our contention is that there is a good deal
embodied in the name chosen for an organization, eg.

- Is the name used related to a person? If so, how?
- What does the organization's name stand for or represent?
  (eg. The Carl Jung Clinic, the Betty Ford Clinic)
- Is the name used as, or adopted from, metaphor or concept?
  (eg. Gingerbread, Nafsiyat)
- Does the name contain a literal description of its activities?
  (eg. Devontown Women's Counselling Centre, International
  Institute for Counselling and Professional Development)
- Is the name an acronym?
- Does the name define geographical area of location or work?
  (eg. The Norwich Centre, the Leicester Counselling Project)
- Does the name imply its client community? Compare for ex-
  ample the terms Devontown Student Counselling Service and
  Devontown University Counselling Service. The latter service
  may see anyone in the University, not just the students.
- Does the name state its philosophic intention? (eg. 'Counsel-
  ling for All')

Given the potential importance of the name of organizations,
occasional attention may have to be brought to the changing
nature of society or the changing patterns of client use within the
agency and a resultant need to change the name. One such classic
example is that of the (originally named) Marriage Guidance

Council which in recent years has changed its name to Relate. The changing pattern of adult relationships within society and the attitude towards such relationships transformed slowly over the decades from the 1940s to the 1980s. The organization explicitly acknowledged these changes in living patterns and attitudes when it changed its name. It also, at the same time, was able to make explicit its own professional intentions through the choice of its new term, ie. to work with either individuals or couples, hetero-sexual or homosexual, concerned about the quality of their intimate relationships.

For older organizations, changes of name can prove more complicated procedures. The more established an organization, the harder it may be to change because of the power of tradition, and the increasingly rigid nature of the developed bureaucracy and the consolidated patterns of professional practice.

Liaison with other Agencies
This is another responsibility that originates from those charged with the management function of a project. As with other facets of representation of the agency to the outside world, liaison with other organizations has to be conducted appropriately, profession-ally and with sensitivity.

We know of one episode where members of a new organization contacted the manager of another counselling agency to arrange to meet to introduce themselves and their work. They also wished to consult the older established organization on ideas for ways forward with their own development and, recognizing their pro-fessional need in this, offered to pay a nominal consultancy fee for the meeting. Subsequently, the dates for the meeting had twice to be cancelled and rearranged by the requesting organization, causing a certain irritation to the manager of the established body. When they eventually did meet, the representative turned up 15 minutes late, was not the person expected but their partner (who had previously been a client of the organization), and who then consumed one-and-a-half hours talking in an over-generalized and non-specific way using conversation peppered with allusions to gossip and difficulties in the organization. Very little clear informa-tion was given. The representative was also not at all clear what help was required as requested in the first phone call! No acknowledgement of the previous fee negotiations were made, nor a fee offered. The lateness of the representative's arrival, combined with the rambling, time-consuming nature of their conversation, needless to say left the established manager feeling frustrated, angry and abused. The result is obvious. The new organization was never referred to or used.

Management Committees, Advisory Groups and Boards of Trustees

Many counselling organizations have a committee or advisory group generally comprised of significant local people and some people within the organization to 'oversee' the organization's work. The explicit, and indeed, noble intentions behind having such committees will include some of the following:

- a body that ensures on behalf of the public that the overall organization remains consistent with its objectives and is operated within legal, financial and ethical parameters
- a respectable front for the organization
- a group who can muster local political persuasion when necessary
- a fund-raising body
- a medium or conduit between the local society and the agency
- a permission-giving body in relation to major changes in policy, financial structure, focus, etc.
- a forum for discussion of organizational issues confronting the agency
- an 'overseeing' board concerned to ensure the competent and legal management of the agency
- a group of enthusiasts for and on behalf of the service
- a reference/advisory group for the manager
- a body having the ultimate authority to influence policy, to hire and fire, to impose financial decisions, etc.
- a think-tank
- moral supporters of the work.

In many instances, management committees may not have explicit statements of task expectations or indeed, 'contracts'. The persons invited to join such committees may also be members of other public bodies and will consequently bring their expectations and experiences gained elsewhere to this new setting.

The composition, structure and remit of management/advisory committees are all tasks that have to be devised and overseen by the manager in the first instance. Given the wide variety of purposes deigned appropriate and listed above for management/advisory committees and bearing in mind the vast spectrum of counselling and psychotherapy services this book might be consulted by, considerable challenge has been experienced in writing meaningfully and usefully on this subject! The chemistry of purpose, personality and ongoing processes will be unique to each organization.

Having listed the wide variety of purposes above, some consideration now follows as to the composition of such groups. A range of ideas are listed that will hopefully stimulate consideration of whose presence would be most valuable.

A dilemma for managers in making initial selections and issuing invitations is that posed by the split between choice of personality and role/organizational representation. A particular person who exhibits desirable qualities may be very attractive whatever their other affiliations. On the other hand, local politicians, business people, representatives of local organizations, etc. might prove desirable to the counselling agency because of their experience, their connections, their knowledge and so on. The choice of selection is thus crudely split between personality and role function. In practice, this division is not often as stark as depicted and combinations of the two may often emerge, eg. 'I wonder if Mr or Mrs So and So would want to be involved, they are sympathetic to organizations such as ours and hold a responsible role professionally . . .'.

If considered from a role-determined perspective, the following might be worthy of consideration:

- local politicians
- local representatives of business
- professional colleagues in statutory organizations
- professional colleagues in voluntary organizations
- previous clients
- counsellors from within the organization
- representatives from the health sector, doctors, psychiatrists
- representatives from referring agencies.

Insurance

The insurance needs of an agency will generally fall into the following categories:

(a) insurance of the building (fire, damage, etc.)
(b) contents insurance (against theft, damage, etc.)
(c) insurance of employees (accidental injury)
(d) insurance to cover any legal actions taken against the organization by dissatisfied clients.

Counselling bureaux situated within larger host organizations may enjoy the wider benefit of the insurance arrangements put in place by the host body. Counselling services in hospitals, GP practices and in colleges might thus be advantageously placed.

However, managers of such facilities would be well advised to ensure that all aspects of the host organization's arrangements do, in fact, cover their own particular requirements. For example, if the counselling agency uses volunteers, are they covered by the arrangements applying to contracted and salaried staff? Would such staff be protected in the event of client-led legal actions? Managers need to attend to these detailed points, having an eye for the differences of operation between their particular unit and the overall organization. These very differences of operation might lead to gaps in the insurance provision requiring attention.

For counselling services structured as stand-alone organizations (covering the wide range of individual independent practices to EAPs, the telephone helplines to community counselling bodies and so on), all aspects of insurance will require thorough investigation and subsequent implementation.

Advice on insurance matters can be obtained via the following organizations:

- insurance agents
- advisers to small businesses
- the British Association for Counselling, 1 Regent Place, Rugby CV21 2PJ. Telephone 01788 550899
- the National Council for Voluntary Organizations. Telephone 0171 713 6161.

Readers may also consult Jenkins, P. (1997) *Counselling, Psychotherapy and the Law*. London: Sage.

Key Points

Introduction

- Consider the importance of the creation of the therapeutic space.
- Changes of work emphasis, crises, team size and so on will require constant attention and modification.

Location and Premises

- Consider the location of the agency and likely implications.
- Ensure appropriate access routes, signposting, etc.
- Consider effects of internal decor and style.
- Test the facilities for accessibility and mobility.

Safety and Maintenance

- Named responsible personnel.
- Job and task specifications.
- Check building against local authority, fire and employer regulations and seek advice where appropriate.

Staffing Structures

- Documentation and diagrams depicting working roles and relationships between them and flow of work can be helpful to everyone in the organization.
- Construct appropriate mechanisms for communication, up, down, across and outside the agency.
- Use the service of a mentor/supervisor for the manager.

Facilitating the Client's Progress through the Agency

- Clear conceptions of client progress, from first point of contact to exit, are helpful to all concerned.
- Operating procedures to effect this process between colleagues require putting in place and job descriptions detailed accordingly.
- Clarity of fees negotiation and collection is required.

Going Public: Promotion and Advertising

■ Disseminating accurate information about the agency is an important task that has educational, informational and orientational implications.

■ Promotion and advertising can be achieved through a variety of mechanisms including talks, posters, leaflets, visits to particular groups, newspapers, articles, radio snippets, etc.

■ Promotional literature might usefully be produced in relationship with advertising agencies though decision on publications choice and content must remain with the counselling organization.

■ Different promotional mechanisms and language(s) might be required for different groups and purposes (client groups, referrers, etc.).

■ Pace advertising in relation to client flow and agency resources.

■ Naming the agency appropriately is an important task.

Liaison with other Agencies

■ Contact making needs to be professionally established.

■ Prepare information for presentation (possibly through role play and simulations).

■ Send an informed representative.

■ Establish the length of the interview and respect the other's time pressures.

Management Committees, Advisory Groups and Boards of Trustees

■ Consider carefully the purpose of establishing such bodies.

■ Consider a form of statement or constitution for its work and procedures.

■ Delegates invited to join the board need to reflect particular aspects of society as defined by the work of the agency.

Insurance

■ Ensure the agency is covered by insurance!

■ Consult appropriate expertise in professional and public bodies.

3

Staff Recruitment and Selection

Staffing a counselling service raises a number of management issues which have standard human resource management solutions that may not be familiar to non-human resource management (HRM) specialists. In this chapter we are going to examine the recruitment, selection and training of staff for a counselling service. The management principles are applicable to counselling services of all sizes and are not a function of the form of the service.

Best practice suggests that there is a standard procedure that needs to occur if appropriate staff are to be recruited, selected

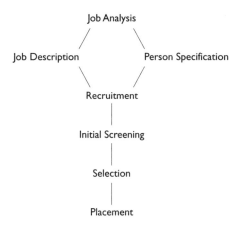

Figure 3.1 *From Job Analysis to Placement*

and appointed. (Recruitment is the generation of applicants for a post and selection is the process of selecting a candidate from amongst the applicants.) Figure 3.1 sets out this standard best practice procedure. The broad meaning of each of the sequential steps and the logic of the process is probably obvious, so we will go on immediately to look in some detail at the steps in the process.

Job Analysis

Before someone can be selected to fill a post the counselling organization needs to be clear what the job entails – the job analysis. When the job has been analysed the information gathered can be used to produce a job description that specifies what the job entails, and a person specification that sets out the qualities and skills that the post holder needs in order to carry out the job specified in the job description. In the case of a counselling agency, job analysis will require that the purpose of the agency is clearly understood and agreed. In a sense this requires that the agency can agree the service or services that are being offered to the clients, thus the agency needs to be clear about its mission and what this implies in terms of the services offered.

It would be all too easy to assume that all the agency had to do was to recruit and select able counsellors. Clearly the tasks that have to be performed in a counselling agency are not just counselling, there will also have to be administration, management, policy making, record keeping, research, training and teaching amongst a whole range of potential tasks. Thus in the job analysis there may well be a whole range of tasks in addition to counselling, even for those who are employed primarily as counsellors: for example, the Sherwood Psychotherapy Training Institute in its Code of Ethics and Professional Practice has a section on 'Continued Development' which requires '. . . continued . . . professional development through any or all of the following: personal therapy, regular supervision, further training, research, publication.' (Sherwood Psychotherapy Training Institute Ltd, 1996) An agency may also look for research, teaching and writing skills in its counsellors.

Best practice for job analysis suggests that the greater the number of sources consulted the greater the validity and completeness of the information obtained. Sources of information could include:

- the current post incumbent
- their manager
- other members of the incumbent's role set
- technical experts, advisors and consultants
- existing written records
- research on the qualities of successful counsellors.

There are numerous appropriate ways that this information can be gathered from the sources, eg.:

- semi-structured and structured interviews
- questionnaires
- checklists
- self report procedures (eg. diaries)
- reading of appropriate research literature.

The information gathered in job analysis has a number of uses, for example it can be used for:

- production of a job description
- production of a person specification
- job design
- job evaluation
- performance appraisal
- personnel selection
- training.

The structure shown in Figure 3.1 is particularly appropriate when an existing member of staff is being replaced or an additional staff member is being recruited, but the analysis can be much more than the analysis of an existing post or type of post. When a counselling organization is being set up, or expanded, or is changing the services that it offers, or at any point in time, the organizational structure can be examined to check that the organization 'fits' its environment (which is likely to be changing all of the time). If an agency is to be successful on an ongoing basis it will need to review regularly the services that it provides and how it provides these services. This review implies an agency organization design element which is both 'what is this agency?' and 'what should this agency be in order to best meet our evolving vision and strategy and the needs of actual and potential clients?' Thus job analysis is both 'what is this job?' and 'what should this job be?' – analysis and design.

The basic information required in job analysis would be:

■ title
■ relationships with other staff members
■ job content
■ working conditions
■ performance standards/objectives
■ other relevant information
■ human requirements, eg. gender, sexual orientation, race.

We suggested that a possible source of information in developing job analysis was research on the qualities of successful counsellors. There has been a great deal of research done on the qualities of a good counsellor or therapist. The results have been singularly unhelpful. The only result that stands out clearly is that 'it is the relationship between the client and . . . [counsellor] . . . more than any other factor, which determines the effectiveness. . . . ' (Clarkson, 1995).

Another common-sense result that emerges from research is that different styles of counselling and therapy result in the client and counsellor relating in very different ways, but there is no clear evidence that one style of counselling or therapy can be seen to be better than others (for a discussion of this see O'Leary, 1992).

Research thus offers little advice for job analysis that can be included in a person specification other than the need to investigate the way that candidates for counselling posts relate to clients, and even then the work summarized by O'Leary (1992) suggests that different counselling styles relate in differing but equally successful ways. The research findings do not, however, prevent agencies from advertising for counsellors trained in a particular therapeutic orientation, eg. psychodynamic, person-centred.

Job Description

The job description will emerge from the job analysis and requires sufficient detail that the post holder will know what is expected of them.

Counselling

- duration, eg. brief therapy/counselling. Much counselling within GP practices and in Employee Assistance Programmes (EAPs) is within a 6–10 session framework; or elsewhere long-term therapy/counselling for often one or more years
- client group, eg. couples, adolescents, women
- presenting problems, eg. general, HIV, debt, bereavement, relationships.

Education and training   For many agencies staff members will be expected to take part in education and training, eg. many university agencies run listening skills, racial awareness and stress management courses for students, academics and administrative staff. Staff may also provide training for their colleagues in the organization. In many counselling agencies where counsellors/listeners/supporters are taken on with little or no training the agency is to a considerable extent a training organization, eg. Relate, who provide relationship counselling, train all of their counsellors within the organization; other similar examples are Cruse, who provide bereavement counselling and Victim Support, who provide support for the victims of crime.

Administration

- client records and appointments
- annual agency reports
- publicity
- course development, administration and delivery
- recruitment and selection of staff
- appraisal of colleagues
- financial management

Policy making   Membership of the agency's directorship, steering committee or policy-making body.

Liaison/external political role   Contact with the stakeholders of the organization, eg. trustees, funding bodies (eg. local authorities, university finance committees), client groups (eg. a university agency will almost certainly liaise with the Students' Union). Under this heading it is a good idea to remember that there are both internal and external stakeholders and to then brainstorm who the stakeholders are, both actual and potential. A significant element of the process of running an organization is the interaction with the internal and external stakeholders.

Secretarial/reception   An agency will require some reception and secretarial skills even if the agency is not big enough for these to be specialist roles. Usually Reception is the client's first contact with the counselling organization and the interaction with the client needs to be professionally and appropriately handled. For example, university porters are often used by distressed students as the first line of pastoral care, even though that is not normally thought of as part of their duties. Similarly an agency receptionist may well find clients starting to use them as the first line of pastoral/counselling care, with clients starting to tell their story.

This is a long list, and any one post holder may well not have all of the listed elements as part of their job, but they do need to know their job description. If the job analysis is not completed thoroughly then an appropriate job description cannot be drawn up, an appropriate person specification cannot emerge and the chance of a good appointment is reduced.

Person Specification

When the job has been analysed and a job description produced based on the analysis, then a person specification can be produced. The person specification is a description of the qualities, training, therapeutic orientation (psychodynamic, person-centred, Gestalt, etc.), experience and qualifications that a person will need in order to fill successfully the role set out in the job description. The person specification feeds into the recruitment stages of the process as potential clients need to know not only what the job entails (the job description), but also whether they meet the criteria for a potentially successful applicant. The full job description and person specification should normally be sent to all the applicants.

Two Case Studies

Case one   A commercial Employee Assistance Programme organization (PPC), who provide short-term counselling (amongst other assistance services) for the self-referred employees of client organizations.

PPC have a number of criteria that their clinical affiliates (counsellors) have to meet. They must hold a professional qualification in one of the following areas:

- Chartered or clinical psychologist
- Psychiatric social work (or, social work with experience in community mental health or chemical dependency)
- Community psychiatric nursing
- British Association for Counselling accreditation
- British Psychology Society accreditation

For all the above there is an additional requirement of three years post-qualification experience to ensure that the qualification is more than a paper qualification without matching practical experience. Applicants who do not meet the above criteria can satisfy the alternative criteria of holding a recognized counselling/therapy qualification plus 500 hours of clinically supervised practice.

Applicants are also expected to have

- an ability to complete a high-quality comprehensive assessment
- a high level of counselling skill and interest in brief, focused therapy
- a knowledge of local resources
- an ability to respond appropriately to crises
- an interest in organizational dynamics.

This person specification specifies appropriate professional qualifications, experience of supervised work with clients and finally outlines some other necessary qualities (assessment, brief therapy, local resource knowledge, etc.). PPC refer to this person specification as their acceptance criteria. The criteria are frequently reviewed to ensure that they are in line with the developing nature of their organization and the changes in their client base and evolving client needs.

Case Two A county counselling scheme for GP practices. This scheme has a clear person specification which is reproduced in Table 3.1.

Table 3.1   *A Specification for a GP Counselling Scheme*

	Essential	Desirable
Qualification	A recognized counsellor training/formal course of theoretical study Eligible for BAC accreditation or equivalent	A health professional qualification
Knowledge	Understanding of the role of the counsellor in primary care Understanding of the constraints of counselling in general practice	Knowledge of inter-agency networking
Experience	Working with a wide range of clients Considerable experience of supervised practice.	Working in a primary health care setting Multidisciplinary team working
Skills	Ability to organize own time and caseload effectively Good communication skills, both written and verbal	Supervisory skills Audit skills Research skills

Source: North Derbyshire Health and South Derbyshire Health, 1995

Applicants are sent a booklet which covers : The Role of the Counsellor, the Contract, Supervision, Criteria for Employment, Code of Ethics, Insurance, Primary Health Care Teams, Training, Training Placements and Appendices covering Job Description for the Role of Counsellors, Contract for the Employment of a Counsellor in General Practice, Person Specification, BAC Accreditation Criteria, Indemnity Insurance and Protocol for Counselling Service to be Provided within a General Practice. The Authority simply states that to be eligible for employment the counsellor must fulfil the standard criteria of the person specification.

We have by implication so far been discussing organizations that hire trained/qualified counsellors. There are also agencies that recruit untrained persons who are suitable to become counsellors and then train them within the agency, eg. Cruse, Relate and Victim Support. The process of job analysis, job description, person specification is just the same as in the appointment of qualified counsellors.

Recruitment

Recruitment is the process of getting appropriately qualified candidates to apply for the post. Potential candidates need to be aware of the post and so the post needs to be advertised in an appropriate medium where potential applicants will be aware of the vacancy. Advertisements can be placed in a wide variety of media:

- newspapers and professional journals
- noticeboards in counselling and therapy training organizations
- newsletters of training organizations.

Essentially the question is, 'where will suitable potential applicants see that we have a vacancy?'

Many agencies may find that potential staff will approach the organization even though there has been no recruitment advertising; thus, for example, Rape Crisis Centres, Cruse, Victim Support may well be able to recruit staff from former clients or from members of the public presenting themselves and expressing an interest.

With the mushrooming growth of counselling training courses there are a large number of people who are training and looking to gain practical experience, or who are required by their training course to gain practical counselling experience. Increasingly such students are approaching agencies. This has led to a problem for some agencies, that there is a high turnover of staff, leading to a high resource cost in training.

People responding to a recruitment advertisement or volunteering will need to demonstrate their suitability for the post. The normal initial stage is to require an application form that seeks information on how the applicant meets the person specification in relation to education, training, experience and personal qualities. Application forms can be designed based on the person specification and would normally be distributed with a job description so that the potential applicant can self-evaluate whether they fit the person specification and whether the job is one for which they wish to apply. The potential applicant's decision whether to apply, based on their response to the person specification and the job description, is the first stage of selection. Thus a comprehensive and carefully designed person specification and job description is an important part of ensuring a good appointment, by eliminating inappropriate candidates even before application.

When applications have been received, the agency can do an initial screening and draw up a short list. From the material submitted by applicants, CVs, application forms and covering letters, candidates can be evaluated with regard to how well they meet the person specification.

Selection

After recruitment and initial screening the short-listed candidates enter the selection process. Research shows clearly that there are a number of invalid and unreliable methods of selection, which strangely are popular, and a number of best practice methods that are much more reliable, although they are often more expensive in terms of making good appointments (Muchinsky, 1986). The cost of various selection methods should be set against the cost of making a poor appointment, eg. expensive training will be wasted on a poor appointment. Many organizations use cheap selection methods and then have to pay the high price of a poor appointment, which includes all the costs of making a replacement appointment.

The terms 'validity' and 'reliability' have important and distinct meanings. Validity means that the selection method does actually indicate/measure the ability to fulfil the job description satisfactorily; the method is a valid predictor of job performance. Reliability means that the selection method will select candidates who will succeed and reject candidates who will fail and that the decision does not depend on the selector who is using the selection technique.

The range of selection techniques available normally includes:

- interviews
- work samples
- situational exercises
- biographical information (Bio-data)
- peer assessment

- self-assessment
- assessment centres
- letters of reference
- graphology.

Interviews

Interviews are the most widely used method of selection despite the research (Herriot, 1987) that clearly shows that unstructured interviews are hardly more successful than using a pin to choose candidates from a list – they have very low validity. If interviews are structured then they have higher validity. To structure interviews each candidate is asked exactly the same questions, using identical wording, in the same order, and their replies are scored against previously agreed answers. Without structure it is very difficult to compare candidates in any meaningful way. The questions must clearly cover at least the aspects of the person specification.

There are a number of well-known problems with interviews. Without structure and interviewer training there is little chance that equal candidates will be evaluated as equals – this is called inter-rater reliability. Interviewing is a skill and both validity and reliability increase if interviewers receive training.

Another problem with interviews is that interviewers often form an early impression of the candidate in the first three or four minutes of the interview and then spend the rest of the interview noting evidence that confirms their early view and minimizing, or failing to perceive, evidence that contradicts their early view. Candidates can also be stereotyped, where the candidate is 'recognized' as an archetype with all the expected characteristics, even though they may have only one or a few of the characteristics.

Whilst interviews are unlikely to be a good selection method, unless structured, they do serve other useful purposes. They allow the exchange of information (there may be better ways of doing this via printed material), and give the candidate the opportunity to seek information that was not contained in the job description and the person specification. If the interviewer(s) and the interviewee will be working together then the interview gives them both the opportunity to assess whether they could have a good working relationship together.

Recent literature suggests that interviews are largely the place where psychological contracts of employment are formed and negotiated, where each party forms expectations of the other, where details outside any contract of employment or job description are negotiated.

If interviews are to be used as a selection method the agency needs to be clear:

- What is the purpose of the interview?
  - assessment of the candidate
  - giving and receiving information
  - induction to the counselling agency
  - personal compatibility
  - psychological contracting.
- What is the structure?
  - unstructured
  - semi-structured
  - structured.
- What is the ratio of interviewers to interviewees?
  - individual (1:1) – one interviewer, one interviewee
  - tandem (2:1) – two interviewers, one interviewee
  - panel (N:1) – a number greater than two interviewers, one interviewee
  - cascade (1:1, sequential) – a series of one-to-one interviews
  - group (N:N) – a group of interviewers meeting with a group of interviewees.
- What interview style?
  - frank and friendly
  - problem solving
  - stress strategy – giving the candidate a 'hard time'
  - sweet and sour – one (or some) interviewer(s) is 'sweet' and one (or others) is 'sour'.

At the interview every interviewer should have read, and have with them

- the job description
- the person specification
- the interviewee's application form, CV, covering letter
- the interview plan or structure and the agreed response plan.

Interviews are a suspect selection device, even when structured, as indicated by their low validity, so best practice recommends that reasons other than selection should be borne in mind, and that the interview should only be part of the selection process.

References
Research, as reported by Muchinsky (1986) has clearly shown that personal references have very low validity as a selection device. This is hardly surprising when the candidate chooses the referees; they are hardly likely to offer references that are not supportive or that contradict information given on the application form or CV. Previous employers' references may at least confirm previous employment history and other matters of fact. Users of references for selection may care to bear in mind the humorous suggestion that if you want to get rid of an employee then you write a glowing reference and if you want to keep them you write a damning reference!

Work Samples and Situational Exercises
The distinction between these two selection methods is fuzzy (Muchinsky, 1986) but in essence they are methods that allow job applicants to demonstrate practically their abilities and suitability for the job.

A counselling example would be to require applicants to provide an unedited tape of them working with a client (whose permission to use the tape had been sought and given). The Counselling Service of Sheffield University uses this method as part of the selection process when selecting part-time counsellors. Perhaps, a little like letters of reference, the candidate is hardly likely to submit a tape that shows them in anything but a favourable light, but an hour's counselling would be a long time to conceal bad counselling practice! This method certainly helps the selection of candidates who are 'good enough'.

Some counselling training organizations provide examination candidates with a live client and listen to the tape of the resulting initial counselling session. Again there are problems of confidentiality, together with problems of 'performance nerves'. This approach only gives evidence directly about how the counsellor is in the initial session and leaves open to speculation how the counsellor would be in later, and perhaps much later, sessions.

Hearing the candidate working in an initial session is particularly appropriate when the agency specializes in short-term counselling and/or brief therapy.

If the post is not for a counsellor but is for a counselling organization's manager or administrator or includes duties other than counselling, then there are standard situational exercises like in-tray exercises and leaderless group discussions that allow the demonstration of interpersonal, diagnostic, prioritizing, oral and persuasion skills (Muchinsky, 1986). Secretarial/reception posts could include typing tests and telephone skills.

Work sample and situational exercises give candidates the opportunity to demonstrate their skills. Studies have shown (Muchinsky, 1986) that the validity of these selection methods is between moderate and high, but much depends on the appropriateness of the samples and exercises chosen, or their design.

Bio-Data

This selection method, which has a high level of validity, is only viable for large organizations making repeated appointments to the same type of post. A multibranch agency might find this a viable method for selecting branch managers or administrators. 'The rationale behind biographical data . . . is that the activities, interests, and behaviours we exhibit in our past are predictive of what we will do in the future' (Muchinsky, 1986). The method is basically that a list of biographical questions are developed and the answers compared with desired selection criteria. Those questions found to be predictive are used in subsequent selection procedures. The candidates fill in the developed questionnaire. The validity of bio-data has been found to be very high, but it does need a large sample of people to develop an appropriate questionnaire.

Peer Assessment

Groups of peers can assess each individual member in one of three standard ways: peer nomination, where each individual nominates the best member of the group in terms of the way that the individual fulfils each selection criterion set out in the person specification; peer ranking, where peers rank individuals against criteria; and peer rating, where peers rate individuals on a scoring scale for the given criterion.

These approaches show only modest validity, but may be regarded as relatively undistorted by any efforts of candidates to present themselves to selection assessors or superiors in a favourable light. Clearly the method can only be used when the peers are well known to one another, and is thus more suited to selection for promotion, or new posts within the agency, from amongst existing employees.

Self-assessment

Applicants' self-assessment has been shown to have low validity as a predictor of job performance. At best it can only supplement other selection techniques, including curriculum vitae.

Assessment Centres

This is a method of selection where applicants are assessed in groups of 10 to 20 over the course of one or two days by a group of trained assessors. They are usually used in selection for managerial/supervisory positions and as part of promotion assessments. The format is normally a set of tests and exercises, for example, interviews, group discussions, in-tray tests and paper and pencil psychological tests. Assessment centres have one of the highest levels of validity of any personnel selection methods, which is hardly surprising as they combine a number of single selection methods into an overall assessment. When used to assess suitability for promotion, assessment centres are particularly effective.

Graphology

Research on graphology has failed to show that handwriting analysis has any validity as a selection method. Handwritten application forms or covering letters will tell you more about the candidate's pen than about their suitability for a post in a counselling service and will leave the selectors with the possible problems of reading the handwriting!

Criminal Records

Dependent on the nature of the work that the successful applicant will be doing, the agency may want to check out whether the applicant has a criminal record that would disqualify them from appointment; clearly agencies working with children would not want to employ paedophiles.

There is one formal way in the UK that a check can be made. Candidates can be asked to have a search made of criminal records kept by the police so that they can produce written evidence that they do not have any relevant criminal record. By law the police have to make the results of the search available to the applicant within four weeks of receiving the application.

The agency cannot directly obtain the applicant's police record. The applicant has to visit a police station, obtain an Enforced Subject Access Enquiry form and, using this form, apply for a copy of their Prosecution/Conviction Record. If the applicant has no record, they will receive a letter stating this. If the applicant does have a record then the letter will set out the details. The Data Protection Act 1998, which will become law on 25 October 1998, will probably restrict the availability of criminal records, although it seems likely that they will still be available where applicants are seeking to work with the vulnerable (children, the mentally ill, the elderly and similar groups).

Some local authorities are currently prepared to offer a service where they undertake a search into an applicant's criminal record. The authority can apply directly to the police without having to do it through the applicant. The police can refuse on the grounds that it is not necessary or appropriate that the records are made available to the authority. Agencies may well find that authorities will not be prepared to make this service available. The situation from October 1998 is still unclear.

Agencies wishing to check criminal records from October 1998 could contact the Data Protection Registrar for details of how that is possible. The information is likely to be available from late June 1998 when the Act will probably have completed its passage through Parliament. The telephone number of the Registrar's very helpful enquiry service is given at the end of Chapter 4 of this book (see p. 74).

The only other way of checking records, used by many commercial organizations, is to use a private investigation agency where a fee is paid and no questions are asked.

Conclusions on Selection

Best practice suggests that a number of selection methods are used for an appointment as any one method by itself does not have high validity. A single selection method is unlikely to lead to a successful appointment. In this chapter we have tried to introduce the reader to good practice in selection. Where more detail is required we refer the reader to Muchinsky (1986), or to a chartered occupational psychologist specializing in selection.

4

Ensuring Competent, Professional and Safe Practice

In this chapter we are going to take up and examine five themes or characteristics. We examine whether the counselling organization is competent, professional, safe, appropriate and accountable. We examine the need for, the existence, the implementation and the improvement of each of these themes or characteristics. In effect we are discussing the auditing of the counselling service. Alternatively we could see this chapter as being about effectiveness (doing the right thing) and efficiency (doing it right).

To begin we will sketch out the landscape, the meaning of the themes, so that the reader can understand why they are important and whether they are important given the reader's position, interests and responsibilities. The remainder of the chapter will discuss the topics in greater depth.

Competence The difference between competence and professionalism is not clear and obvious, and the reader may well think that we have made an artificial distinction, have drawn a line between topics that are essentially a single topic. However, we think that there is a useful and important distinction. We will discuss competence in terms of the quality of the services or products provided, and how quality is defined and by whom.

When we discuss who should define quality we will do so within a stakeholder framework. Stakeholder analysis will be used in a number of places within the book as a powerful tool for thinking about organizations.

Professionalism Here we will discuss whether the services are produced in a professional way. Thus the distinction is between the quality of the product (competence) and the quality of the production process used in producing the quality services. Professionalism will be discussed in terms of conformity to appropriate codes of ethics and professional practice.

Safety This concerns the physical, psychological and emotional welfare of the clients of the counselling organization and is covered within the codes of ethics and professional practice. The safety of the staff is partly covered by the codes, but it will also be discussed in Chapter 6 within the discussion of burnout and vicarious traumatization (the long-term impact that counselling and therapy work can have on counsellors and therapists).

Appropriateness Here we will briefly discuss *what* services are provided by the counselling agency, and for *whom* and whether the agency has the resources that are appropriate to provide the services.

Accountability Here we will discuss who the counselling service is accountable to and how it can report. The 'who' part will again use a stakeholder framework.

Competence

Our first problem is to define what constitutes a competent counselling organization, and perhaps *who* defines a competent organization; which of the stakeholders that define the organization should define competence? The obvious candidates are the clients and/or the staff of the agency.

The clients could define competence in terms of whether their experience of the service that they receive is what they want. Here we have competence defined in the way that quality is often defined in business management literature (see, for example, Bank, 1992), as the extent to which the service received was equal to, greater than, or less than expected. Conformance to specification would be an alternative perspective, where the specification was the contract that had been agreed for their counselling.

Clients are rarely experts in counselling or therapy and thus their expectations are formed in an ill-defined way by what they have read and heard about counselling. We may expect, but we don't know, that this expectation is formed by discussions of counselling that appear in the popular media, and what the agency says about its services. One way of testing whether the clients' experience of the agency was of competence would be to ask them to fill in a questionnaire at the end of their course of counselling sessions. This approach is not uncommon, especially among Employee Assistance Programme (EAP) services.

An alternative definition of competence could be framed by the counselling agency rather than by the clients. Competence here is likely to be a function of a number of professional factors – are the staff competent (are they good counsellors)?; have they received appropriate training?; do they practise competently, in the sense of using their counselling skills well?; do they keep appropriate records with care?; do they competently fulfil the other terms in their contract as teachers, researchers, scholars and administrators?

How can we assess whether staff are competent in this organization-defined way? Normally assessors do not sit in on counselling sessions or observe through one-way screens, but both are possible although the presence of an assessor would change the field (Yontef, 1993) and thus the whole process of interaction between the counsellor and client. The video or audio taping of sessions also allows for assessment of the counsellor's competence, but a single tape is no more than a sample which brings with it the problem that attaches to small samples, that is, the high probability of them being unrepresentative of the whole population of counselling sessions completed by the counsellor or team of counsellors (McCall, 1996).

Assessment of competence is initially carried out through the staff selection process (see Chapter 3) and subsequently through the process of clinical supervision. However, supervision is not normally set up as an assessment process and there is usually a contract of confidentiality that limits the use of supervision to check on competence, even if the supervision is internal to the agency.

If staff training is offered internally within the organization then there is an opportunity not only to build and develop competence, but also for the trainer to act in an assessor's role, to monitor the level and development of the individual counsellor's competence. As with supervision, if the trainer is asked to play a double role (in this case as teacher and assessor) then the field is changed and the process of training may be changed and blurred, for example by performance anxiety on the part of the trainee.

Thus far we have written of the assessment of competence in counselling, but we need to remember that the counsellor's contract is likely to include other duties or roles such as administration and client record keeping, working as a trainer, a researcher and possibly a scholar. We suggest that in these roles, that are in addition to, or complement, the process of counselling, competence can be assessed in the same way as is used in other organizations, through appraisal and other standard assessment techniques advocated and researched by management writers (see, for example, Fletcher, 1994). We will discuss best practice for staff appraisals next.

Staff Appraisal

If an agency is to be successful, as competent as it can be, then it needs a motivated, appropriately trained and developed staff. It has long been argued that a staff appraisal system can make a contribution to staff motivation and development. Current literature, for example Randall (1994), suggests that a contingency approach is used in the design of the system so that the system is unique to the situation and nature of the organization; thus, it is argued, there is no single best appraisal system.

An extension of this contingency approach applies to the use of the current literature on appraisal. Most of the literature and recommended best practice is based on profit-making organizations (not the situation of most counselling services, except some commercial EAP organizations) and looks to compare employees either with one another or with some token best or average standard of performance. We speculate that most counselling services are more concerned with developing their staff than with trying to motivate them to be better than the best of their fellow workers.

Standard appraisal systems look to appraise staff for four reasons: reward/payment, potential/promotability, performance and development. Clearly there are overlaps in these four; staff development and performance clearly overlap, as do performance and reward.

Best practice clearly recommends that during any appraisal session only one of the four reasons is covered, otherwise there is role conflict. An appraisal that tried to cover both performance (in relation to the possibility of promotion or a pay increase) and development would fail. No one is going to talk about their weaknesses and their need for development when pay or promotion are also on the menu.

In a counselling service there are likely to be counsellors who counsel and who also manage, administer, teach and research, and staff who do not counsel – administrators, receptionists and secretaries. We have suggested that the appraisal of counsellors as counsellors is difficult. Conventional techniques may, however, be used to appraise them in their non-counselling roles. Those staff members who are not counsellors may be appraised in a conventional way.

Appraisal can be seen as a two-way dialogue in which the agency is involved with the development of the individual, and the individual is involved with the development of the agency. Such mutual involvement is seen to lead to the involvement and motivation of staff (Fletcher, 1994). The two major elements of appraisal systems are 'who appraises?' and 'how?'. There is no single answer to who appraises. The conventional options are seen to be:

(a)   self-appraisal
(b)   peer appraisal
(c)   line manager(s) appraisal
(d)   subordinate appraisal
(e)   appraisal by members of the personnel department
(f)   appraisal by external consultants
(g)   appraisal by the line manager's line manager.

We will comment briefly on alternatives (a) to (d) as the most appropriate for counselling services.

Self-appraisal This is subject to the perceptual problems and tactics of the individual. Research suggests that '. . . on average people thought they were performing better than 75% of their peers' (Fletcher, 1994).

Peer appraisal   This seems to work particularly well when the appraisal is not a competitive process. Peers are often uniquely experienced in how their peers are performing.

Line manager appraisal   This has long been the typical appraiser. However, when staff are working in a number of teams it may give a more rounded view if all of the people who acted as their team leader comment.

Subordinate appraisal   This is a recent development, which seems particularly useful when managers are being appraised, but it may help if the contributions are anonymous.

Recent writing has increasingly suggested that a combination of appraisers may give the best results. A combination of appraisers will help to average out the recognized biases that are present in appraisals by individuals.

There are many methods of appraisal, most of which are unlikely to be appropriate for a counselling service as they approach appraisal from the point of view of comparing appraisees with one another. Thus Graphical Rating Scales, Ranking Procedures, Paired Comparisons and Forced Distributions are not discussed. They may be appropriate for large commercial services. More appropriate methods are those that are linked to behaviour. The two standard methods related to behaviour are: Behaviour Anchored Rating Scales (BARS), where the analysis of critical incidents in the work is used to highlight appropriate and desirable behaviours where the excellence of the appraisee can be indicated on a scale; and Behavioural Observation Scales (BOS) which is similar to BARS, but here the frequency with which the behaviour is observed is noted (from 'never' to 'always'). Both BARS and BOS help facilitate discussion at the appraisal interview by focusing on behaviours related to the job rather than feelings and emotions.

One final method of appraisal revolves around the meeting and making (agreeing) of objectives. This approach is sometimes called Management by Objectives (MBO). Here the appraiser and the appraisee meet to discuss the development of objectives and review performance against previously agreed objectives. This approach is thought to result in better commitment, motivation and performance. The approach gives plenty of scope to examine the development and training needs of the staff.

Readers who wish to read a detailed discussion of appraisal are referred to Cascio (1995) and for a detailed discussion of designing systems to ACAS (1988).

Professionalism and Safety

We distinguish professionalism from competence largely with reference to skill. Competence is about the skills with which staff of the counselling agency operate, for example, how skilful they are as counsellors. Professionalism is different in that we mean it to indicate the extent to which the counsellor and the counselling organization work within a code of ethics and a code of practice.

There are a number of elements that need to be considered when thinking about codes of ethics and practice. The counselling service needs to find or develop appropriate codes; the staff of the service need to sign up to the codes; and the staff and the service need to be monitored or assessed to see that the codes are enacted and inform the practice of the agency and the individuals within it.

All counselling organizations and counsellors should work within a code of ethics and a code of practice. (For a discussion of this imperative see Holmes and Lindley [1991], especially Chapter 9.) In the UK many counselling agencies have adopted or adapted the British Association for Counselling (BAC) Code of Ethics and Code of Practice for Counsellors. The BAC has codes for those using counselling skills who are not counsellors, for counsellors, for counselling supervisors, and for trainers in counselling and counselling skills.

Some agencies may need specialist additions or variations from the BAC codes. An example would be the way that a telephone helpline service requires its counsellors to respond to obscene telephone calls (Sanders, 1993). Another variation could concern rules around confidentiality in a peer counselling service within a police force. In this situation the counsellors are both counsellors and police officers. As counsellors they might subscribe to the BAC codes concerning confidentiality, but as police officers they are bound by their duty to report breaches of the law. Such schemes have addressed this complex issue around confidentiality.

With codes of ethics and practice in place (defining what constitutes professional practice) there is the additional need to monitor or assess the extent to which members of an agency, and the agency itself, do observe and implement the codes in their practice. Here there is a double responsibility – a responsibility on the counselling organization to agree suitable codes and make sure that members of the organization know the codes and understand the implications for their practice, and a second responsibility to ensure that the codes are indeed not only known but are enacted by individual members of the agency and the agency as a whole. This requires an assessment of structure and systems as well as process: do the structure and systems of the agency enact the codes and do the systems operate as defined? This is a systems audit. Assessment of the extent to which individuals enact the codes can be observed through super-vision (for the individual counsellor) and through feedback from clients.

A counselling service may choose to make every client aware of the codes, not only to provide a sense of safety and security for clients, but also so that they will be aware of at least some of the breaches of the codes if they experience them. The BAC Code of Ethics covers the core values and principles. The Code of Practice is the detailed enactment implicit in the Code of Ethics.

The BAC Code of Ethics (1993) for counsellors states:

A.1　Counselling is a non-exploitative activity. Its basic values are integrity, impartiality, and respect. Counsellors should take the same degree of care to work ethically whether the counselling is paid or voluntary.

A.2　Client Safety: All reasonable steps should be taken to ensure the client's safety during counselling.

A.3　Clear Contracts: The terms on which counselling is offered should be made clear to clients before counselling com-mences. Subsequent revisions of these terms should be agreed in advance of any change.

A.4　Competence: Counsellors should take all reasonable steps to monitor and develop their own competence and to work within the limits of that competence. This includes having appropriate and ongoing counselling supervision/consultative support.

One feature that stands out is that the Code refers to the individual counsellor and not to the organization. It could be argued that for an agency to be ethical it is enough that the individual counsellors are ethical in their practice. However, we shall be looking at the way that an agency needs systems and processes to enable the individual counsellors to work ethically and professionally.

Another point that needs to be made is that the BAC distinguishes between counsellors and people using counselling skills. There is a BAC Code of Ethics for each. There is a clear distinction between counselling and using counselling skills. If there is a clear bilateral contract to be a client's counsellor then the Counsellors' Code applies. If, however, skills are being used but there is no bilateral contract, and the role is not that of a counsellor, then the appropriate Code is that for people using counselling skills. This situation could arise in a counselling service for staff who are not counsellors. An agency receptionist could well find people starting to tell their story.

A code of ethics provides a frame of reference within which the counsellors in an organization can work. The detail of how those ethics are enacted is a code of practice. In the next section we are going to examine in some detail the BAC Code of Practice for Counsellors so that we can indicate the systems and processes that an organization needs in order to ensure that its counsellors can and do work ethically and professionally.

Code of Practice for Counsellors: the Counselling Agency's Role

In summing up the previous section, we contend that an agency needs to ensure that it has a code of ethics and a code of practice for its counsellors and the counsellors need to know the codes and have 'signed up' to them. It is our view that this is not enough to ensure ethical and professional practice. The agency has a role in ensuring that counsellors can and do practise ethically and professionally.

The BAC Code is taken as an example of a code that has been widely adopted by counselling organizations, or that has acted as the starting point for the development of codes particularly as they relate to individual practitioners. The BAC Code covers:

(a) Issues of responsibility
to the client: client safety, client autonomy, pre-counselling information, contracting and counsellor competence.
to former clients
to self as counsellor
to other counsellors
to colleagues and members of the caring professions
to the wider community: law, social context.
(b) Counselling supervision/consultative support
(c) Confidentiality: clients, colleagues and others
(d) Confidentiality in the legal process
(e) Advertising and public statements
(f) Research
(g) Resolving conflicts between ethical priorities
(h) The availability of other codes and guidelines relating to counselling.

Having noted that the above Code is for individuals, we will now discuss the role of a counselling service under each of the above headings.

Issues of Responsibility to the Client

Client safety The agency should take care that the client is physically safe; for example, a client who needs to do cathartic work should be able to without the risk of injuring themselves because of inappropriate furniture and equipment. Thus the agency may take care to equip counselling rooms with cushions, tennis racquets, old telephone directories and similar material for anger work. Appropriate training and supervision will also help ensure that the client is physically safe whilst working. The clients' psychological safety needs to be ensured by appropriately trained and supervised staff – an organizational responsibility.

Client autonomy Clients are encouraged to take and retain responsibility for their own life. The counsellor should take responsibility for setting, maintaining and making explicit clear boundaries between counselling and any other relationship with the client. Clients should not be exploited sexually, financially, emotionally, or in any other way, by their counsellor or by the agency. If the agency charges for counselling then it is their duty to ensure that clients are not financially exploited either in terms of the level of fees or the duration of the counselling.

Pre-counselling information   Any publicity material, and all written and oral information should reflect accurately the nature of the services offered by the counselling agency and should include material on fees, if charged, and the training, qualifications and relevant experience of the counsellors. A counselling service should take all reasonable steps to honour undertakings offered in its pre-counselling information. To meet these recommendations the agency has to prepare clearly all its written material so that it conforms to the code of practice that the agency has adopted. This will require that the appropriate CVs of all counsellors are to hand and that these CVs and the publicity and information material made available to potential clients are regularly updated as counsellors receive further training and become more experienced. Clients, especially those using counselling for the first time, are likely to know little about counselling and the training of counsellors, and thus printed information is reassuring and develops appropriate expectations against which the agency, and the service that it provides, can be measured. Accurate, up-to-date and full information about the agency is necessary if it is to use feedback from clients as a form of audit of performance. Before clients can comment on their experience of the organization they need to know what to expect, and what standards are set.

Contracting   A contract needs to be agreed with the client before counselling begins, covering availability, confidentiality (including the client's access to any personal records kept, the availability of these records to others, and the security of such records), the counsellor's expectations of the client (including fees, cancellation of appointments, ending of the counselling relationship and opportunities for subsequent re-contracting). Before the contract is agreed the counsellor also needs to know of any other therapeutic or helping relationships and to agree permission, or not, to confer with these other professionals. Any conflicts of interest also have to be discussed and resolved.

As clients may well be confused and overwhelmed when first meeting their counsellor it is good practice to give a copy of the contract to the client so that there can be no confusion or mis-remembering over what was agreed. Indeed, a copy of the contract can be kept by the agency. An agency may choose to have pre-printed and amendable contracts as many of the elements of the contract will be standard, for example, fees, appointments, cancellations and endings.

The Data Protection Acts of 1984 and 1998 also have implications for a counselling organization in relation to the keeping of client details and records. We will write more about the Data Protection Acts when we come to discuss client confidentiality. For further details see Jenkins (1997) and Sills (1997).

Counsellor competence The counsellor's competence to work with a particular client is a matter of judgement of the counsellor, informed by their training, experience, and doctor as well as their supervisor. To the extent that an organization allocates clients to counsellors in the agency, the agency needs to exercise care that a client is referred to a counsellor who is competent in relation to that client's needs.

Issues of Relationships to Former Clients
Any relationship that a counsellor has with a former client must conform to the service's code of practice, and if there is any doubt then the potential relationship must be taken to supervision.

Responsibility to Self as Counsellor
The BAC Code places responsibility on counsellors for ensuring that they are mentally, emotionally and medically fit to counsel. The agency also has a role in this matter, in that the individual counsellor may at times not have enough self-awareness concerning their fitness, physically, emotionally and psychologically, to counsel. The agency should have a duty of care both for its clients and its counsellors. Supervision may frequently not be enough to cover this duty of care.

The Code also places a duty on counsellors to be appropriately trained and continuously developing professionally. Again, the counselling service has a duty of care to ensure that counsellors are appropriately trained for their work and that clients are offered appropriately trained counsellors.

The Derbyshire Counselling Scheme which places counsellors in GP practices has three separate types of post to cover these issues. They have Qualified Counsellors, with previous experience of working in health and primary care in addition to their counselling training and experience, who have a caseload and are expected to have clinical supervision (a financial contribution towards the cost is made by the Scheme); Trainee Counsellor placements, where trainee counsellors work in a GP practice, with a caseload under the guidance of a mentor (a fully qualified and experienced counsellor already working in the GP practice), in addition to clinical supervision (provided on a weekly basis by the Scheme for groups of trainees); and Professional Development placements for qualified counsellors who have no experience in health and primary care, where there is a caseload, a mentor and clinical supervision (arranged by the trainee).

The BAC Code suggests that counsellors should consider their need for professional indemnity insurance. Given the nature of the work, and the likelihood of the clients replaying their lives in the counselling process, official complaints and even legal claims against counsellors and therapists are a real possibility. The sheer expense of legal assistance presents a strong case for professional indemnity insurance, however trained and professional the counsellor is and strives to be. Organizations may well find that if all their counsellors are covered by the same insurance scheme, there will be a group discount on the premiums. The writers know of at least one such scheme.

Also under this heading the BAC suggests that counsellors need to ensure the adequacy of their own previous and ongoing training. We have written earlier in this chapter about individual professional appraisal, where one of the issues is personal development, training, strengths and weaknesses.

Finally under this heading the BAC talks of a counsellor's responsibility for their own safety. There is little that an organization can do in this respect except to ensure, where possible, that there are other people working in the building whenever clients are being seen. If the nature of the client base is such that violence against counsellors might be expected, then agencies should consider installing panic buttons in counselling rooms.

Responsibility to Other Counsellors

In the BAC Code this section considers the importance of counsellors doing nothing in their work to undermine public confidence in their own work as a counsellor or in other counsellors. It also places a duty on counsellors to address directly misconduct by other counsellors.

Whilst the role of the counsellor is addressed here, there is also a role for the agency, particularly through the counselling service manager, to make provision for counsellor misconduct or complaints procedures. More generally the service needs to set up appropriate bodies or committees to address all breaches of the service code of ethics and professional practice. Clients also need to know how they can lodge a complaint and what the process will be. In contracting with a potential client or in publicity material it needs to be made clear that complaints of breaches of codes can be made and how they are processed. It also needs to be made clear to clients that breaches of codes should be reported to the organization. A clear implication is that the clients should be aware of the codes so that they can know when they have been breached.

Responsibility to Colleagues, Members of the Caring Professions and the Wider Community

The BAC Code suggests that not only do counsellors have a duty to clients to be quite clear what services they are qualified and experienced to offer, but that duty extends to colleagues and members of the caring professions, so that no client is referred to a member of an organization, or to an agency, where it is not appropriate. This requires great care in accepting and making referrals. Here the duty of the agency is to ensure that it knows exactly the training, experiences (and perhaps preferences) of its counsellors, so that appropriate referrals may be made for clients approaching the agency.

Under this section of the Code is the requirement that counsellors are aware of the law and operate within it. Jenkins (1996, 1997) comments that many counselling courses do not include enough law teaching, if any. A counselling agency needs to ensure that it does work within the law that applies to counselling. The management and the counsellors within the agency need to know the relevant law. This training could be through courses or through appropriate reading (see Jenkins, 1997). Again the agency needs, within this topic, to be aware of the provisions of the Data Protection Acts – this will be more fully covered when we discuss confidentiality.

Counselling Supervision/Consultative Support

All counsellors should have supervision, the amount of which will vary with their workload and their experience. The BAC view, and that of other professional bodies in the UK, is that all counsellors should receive supervision and that it is not something that you grow too experienced to need. A thoughtful case for supervision is put forward by Bond (1996).

The role of the counselling organization in this respect is to ensure that all counsellors observe this requirement for supervision and possibly to provide the supervision within the agency or to finance outside supervision. The agency may, however, decide that it is the individual counsellor's responsibility to arrange and/or pay for supervision. If the agency decides to provide supervision internally, then good practice requires that the roles of line manager and supervisor are not confused. Indeed it would be best if one person did not fill both roles for any one counsellor. If a line manager also acts as a supervisor then the counsellor should also have supervision from another supervisor. Bond (1996) discusses very clearly the problems that arise from combining the two roles in one person.

Confidentiality: Clients, Colleagues and Others

Most of the clauses under this heading in the BAC Code concern the behaviour of the individual counsellor and do not have any implications for an organization other than to ensure that counsellors know what is included in the code of practice adopted by the agency in relation to confidentiality.

Perhaps the only other requirement of the agency concerns confidentiality of client records. Currently (March 1998) the confidentiality of client records is legally governed by the Data Protection Act 1984. This Act will be replaced on 25 October 1998 by a new Act that will conform to the European Commission General Directive of October 1995. Not all of the details of the new Act are clear until it has passed through Parliament, but some details are clear as they must conform with the EC Directive. As from October 1998 *all* client records may have to be available to clients, if requested, whether they are kept in computers (the current, 1984 Act, situation) or on paper, audio or video, so long as the client's record can be identified (even if by code). Under the 1984 Act all holders of personal records on computers have to register with the Data Protection Agency. Under the 1998 Act it is not currently clear who will have to register and how they will register.

Under the 1998 Act, if an agency is going to show client records to a third party then this has to be recorded with the Registrar, although the name of the third party does not have to be given. This provision will apply if records are going to be shared with a clinical supervisor. Under the 1984 Act only computer-held records were covered by this provision. Counselling services should check with the Registrar from the end of June 1998 for clear details and guidelines. The telephone number of the Data Protection Registrar's very helpful enquiry service is given at the end of this chapter.

The death of a counsellor also raises difficulties around confidentiality. Good practice requires that each counsellor makes provision for how their clients and their records should be treated in the eventuality of the counsellor's death or sudden inability to continue practice. Whoever 'inherits' client records will be bound by the Data Protection Act of 1998. Whatever the reason for the ending of the practice it is good practice for the agency to keep a record of the arrangements made by each counsellor for an abrupt ending of their practice. The agency may even choose to have a policy about sudden endings. For a fascinating discussion about the issues around this topic see Traynor and Clarkson (1996).

The 1984 and 1998 Acts require that personal information should be held securely, using 'proper security'. The BAC Code recommends that all personal files, however kept, should be secure. The security should include not only computer passwords and lock and key, but also the separation of names from records so that records are only identified by some type of code, with the code kept secure and apart from the records.

Confidentiality in the Legal Process

If information about clients is requested by the police and the legal system, the situation can be quite complex. The basic response is that no confidential material should be released in writing, in the form of written records, or orally, unless the police or the courts have a legal right to the material and can show that they have that right. For a fuller discussion of the topic, the reader could turn to Jenkins (1997). Members of the BAC may seek detailed legal advice from the BAC. Alternatively, counselling organizations may wish to retain a solicitor who can advise on this specialist area.

Advertising and Public Statements

The counselling agency equivalent of an individual's obligations under the Code requires that it should always make statements about itself that are accurate and that do not belittle other agencies or other therapeutic/counselling approaches.

Research

Many codes of practice require that individual counsellors should seek their own continued self-development, which may include research. The individual counsellor should only use counselling material for published research if the formal permission of the client(s) has been freely and knowingly given. An agency should exercise great care that material generated within it is not used in such a way as to breach individual client confidentiality. An alternative is that the identity of any client used in published or publicly presented work (research, teaching, conferences) should be adequately disguised. Even then, it is good practice to seek client permission and have the disguise agreed.

Resolving Conflicts between Ethical Priorities

The application of codes of ethics and practice, however well drawn, can still lead to conflicts. An individual counsellor could take such conflicts to supervision, but a counselling organization should ideally have a standards and ethics committee, or a particular external consultant, which can consider and advise on such issues and which can through time build up a body of decisions on ethical matters that is appropriate to the nature of that particular organization. Dependent on the nature of the services offered and the client group, each service may well have unique sets of ethical problems and dilemmas; for example, an HIV counselling service may well have quite distinct ethical dilemmas compared with a service that offers family therapy, or a rape crisis centre.

The discussion above about the way that a counselling organization can ensure professionalism and high standards by the adoption or adaptation of appropriate codes of ethics and professional practice has been based around the Codes of the BAC. Agencies wishing to draw up codes which are appropriate to their particular needs may want to consult the codes drawn up not only by the BAC, which acts as a model for many organizations, but also the codes of a variety of other organizations, particularly those of agencies doing similar work.

The BAC Codes apply to individual counsellors and here we have sought to highlight the implications of such codes for a complete organization (of more than one individual). We have thus tried to spell out the necessary systems for an agency to practise in a professional manner. The BAC also has a publication offering guidelines on good practice for telephone helplines. It also has drawn up Codes of Ethics and Practice for Counselling Skills, Supervisors of Counsellors, and Trainers in Counselling and Counselling Skills.

Appropriateness

In order to discuss appropriateness we need to consider a number of related aspects: the agency mission statement; organizational structure; the school of counselling (person-centred, psychodynamic, etc.); the life experiences of the counsellor; and the presenting problem-specific training of counsellors (counsellors specifically trained to work with the abused/HIV/eating disorders, etc.). These topics will form the basis of the discussion that follows.

If an agency has a mission statement this may specify what client group it aims to service. Thus Alcoholics Anonymous (AA) specifically aims at the client group of alcoholics, as illustrated in their client introductions at meetings, for example, 'My name is Duncan [or whatever] and I am an alcoholic'. What may happen to such a defined organization is that it finds that it is attracting connected but separate client groups. Thus AA found that the relatives of alcoholics also wanted support and counselling, but realized that the resources and meetings of AA were not appropriate to this different work with this different but related client group. AA chose to set up a separate organization specifically targeted at the relatives (initially the wives) of alcoholics, which became Al-Anon for Relatives. When it became clear that the children of alcoholics also had a need, then a further related agency called Alateen was formed, which, whilst related to Al-

Anon, is largely independent and meets a separate need for a specific group of clients.

AA and all its related spin-off organizations is an example of one solution to the evolution of an organization, one way to remain appropriate whilst having and keeping a clear mission. As new clients have emerged AA has developed separate organizations to meet the special needs of the new client groups. An alternative, which they did not follow, would have been to accept the new clients into AA and expand their resources and range of training and expertise, but then the agency would have become less focused and the mission would have been changed implicitly or explicitly. The design of the structure of the organization is one way to ensure that the agency remains appropriate to the needs of the clients that approach it. AA (and its spin-off organizations) is not a conventional counselling service, has not been, and does not wish to be. All of its members are recovering alcoholics and are not professionally trained counsellors employed by a service, and yet the work done clearly is of a therapeutic nature.

When an organization is considering whether it has appropriate resources for its emerging pattern of clients, the discussion may be informed by the school of therapy/counselling practised in the agency. Thus Gestalt therapists or client-centred therapists are likely to feel that the process of therapy or counselling that they offer is not specific and limited to any particular presenting problem. The huge growth of books on working with people with specific presenting problems would suggest that many counsellors hold the view that therapeutic styles determined by 'presenting problem' are appropriate (see, for example, Scott and Stradling (1992), *Counselling for Post Traumatic Stress Disorder*; Draucker (1992), *Counselling Survivors of Childhood Sexual Abuse*). This concern over what resources are appropriate to particular pre-senting problems raises a whole raft of issues around whether the counsellor/therapist can work with a client if the counsellor/therapist has not 'been there' and done their own work. For example, do gay clients need gay counsellors, do abused clients need counsellors who have experienced abuse (or is it enough that they have received training on working with the abused) and can angry clients work on anger with therapists who have not worked on their own anger?

Before a counselling agency can resolve issues of appropriate-ness of its services, it needs to have resolved the following issues:

around its mission; the related issues around its beliefs as to whether specialist training is needed for particular presenting problems; the issues as to whether it believes that counsellors must share their clients' broad situation (gays for gays, alcoholics for alcoholics, women for women, abused for the abused); and finally the issues around whether counsellors/therapists must have had therapy where they have dealt with their own experiences of their clients' problems, for example, anger or abuse. Only when the agency has addressed and resolved these philosophical issues can it then design and maintain, in a changing environment, a system to monitor what an appropriate agency would be.

The organization can monitor its activities in a variety of ways:

Internal environment monitoring What are the presenting problems and revealed problems of the clients with whom they work? Here the agency can design a simple pro-forma which offers a variety of presenting/revealed problems plus a line for 'Any other presenting/revealed problems, please specify.' Using such forms the service can monitor the pattern of clients with whom they have worked and any changes to the pattern or the emergence of new presenting problems.

If a counsellor agrees to work with a client, and continues to work with that client, then this must be done within the codes of ethics and professional practice of the organization. If these are the BAC Codes, or something similar, then the individual counsellor will have reflected on their competence to work with that client and their presenting problem. If on reflection the counsellor decides that it is not appropriate that they or the agency works with this client, then the agency still needs to record who it referred the client on to so that it can subsequently examine the pattern of referrals and make any necessary consequent decisions about its mission, its resources or its training. The appropriateness of the agency can thus be reflected upon.

External environmental monitoring There is no clear division between the internal and external environment that is monitored, as what is monitored in terms of clients and referrals is a reflection of the external environment. However, the agency can reflect on societal trends in order to assess what services they could or should provide. The growing research literature on post-traumatic stress disorder (PTSD) has made it clear that there is a need for counselling agencies to respond to public disasters (like Dunblane, Zeebrugge, King's Cross) by providing counselling services for those traumatized. The growth of bank, building society and post office armed raids has made clear the growing importance of critical incident debriefing. The growing public awareness of child abuse has led to the setting up of telephone helplines. Many other examples could be given of environmental monitoring leading to the awareness of a need to set up or provide services that are appropriate to emerging needs.

Not only does environmental monitoring lead to awareness of emerging needs that an agency may choose to meet, but the growing public awareness of counselling and changing public attitudes towards seeking counselling has resulted in more people seeking counselling. In response there has been an explosion in the number of counsellors and counselling services, hopefully an appropriate response.

Accountability

The last topic in this chapter is accountability. The first question that needs to be answered is 'accountable to whom?'. If we ask who the stakeholders of the organization are, then we have some answer to the question. Let us list the actual or potential stakeholders: funding bodies; clients; the staff of the agency; the home organization, for example, the company who has an internal counselling service as part of its EAP; and client organizations (in the case of commercial EAP companies). Any one agency is unlikely to have everyone on the list, although some may have a longer list.

The clients and staff of a counselling agency might be surprised at the idea that the agency should be accountable to them. The clients probably do their own implicit cost–benefit study for the counselling they received – was what they received worth the cost that they paid, even if that was time and emotion rather than a financial cost? The staff of the agency may well want to know that the resources were appropriately used and that the policy could be justified if not collectively made. In each case an annual report might satisfy their need for accountability. Possible topics for inclusion in an annual report of a student counselling service are clearly set out in Ross (1996), which is a nice example of what might be included in an annual report - it is based on what the service did with its resources during the year.

In the case of funding bodies, home and client organizations, the question may well be 'What are we getting for our money?' or, more commercially, 'What is the rate of return on our expenditure on the counselling service?'. There are no easy answers to these questions and much research suggests that the very nature of the gains from counselling make it difficult to evaluate. How do you put a value on increased happiness, the benefit that comes from learning to be assertive, etc.? (Ross, 1996).

There have been studies completed by commercial organizations on the commercial cost-benefit of counselling services. For example, United Airlines found a benefit-cost ratio for every dollar spent on their counselling services of 16:1, Equitable Life found a ratio of 3:1 and General Motors 2:1. The General Motors study showed that counselling cut lost time by 40 per cent, accidents by 50 per cent and sickness benefits by 60 per cent (Ross, 1996). The commercial benefits can only be estimated, and may still not take into account the benefits to other organizations, for example, if counselling not only reduces sick leave but also reduces the NHS tranquillizer and sleeping tablet bill, then the commercial firm is unlikely to include the benefit to the NHS in its calculation of cost-benefit. There is also the problem of how long the benefits of the counselling need to be incorporated. How do you evaluate the benefits in a life time derived from counselling of a student that enabled them to get a 2.1 degree rather than a third class degree? (Ross, 1996).

Perhaps with accountability we need to ask who wants to know, what do they want to know and how much will it cost to produce the answers? The whole topic of accountability is not only an economic one (even if that is possible) but also a political one. The counselling organization can ask and negotiate with its stakeholders what form of accountability they want, so that what the agency produces (annual reports, quarterly reports, cost-benefit studies, sets of accounts, etc.) meets the agreed requirements. Unless the stakeholders negotiate an agreement with the agency over accountability there is always the risk of providing reports, etc. that do not meet the stakeholders' requirements or that make no economic sense in terms of costing more to produce than the benefit to the stakeholder.

Resources

Details of the Data Protection Acts of 1984 and 1998 and useful publications are available from The Data Protection Registrar, tel: 01625 545745.

5

Daily Working Practices

The consequences of management are very often most visible in the detail of the daily working practices of an organization. The normal, procedural, core activities of the agency must be based on the firm foundations of clear work procedures, known and understood by all colleagues involved. In many circumstances, these behaviours and systems will have grown and developed over time in response to the work demands as interpreted by the personnel involved. A creative tension inevitably exists here between the personalities of the colleagues involved, the dynamic ways they have come to relate in, the decisions and procedures they have evolved over time and the variety of demands presented by clients. In this very detailed sense, no two organizations will be the same, though they might apparently have similar procedures for client reception, placement and so on. Nowhere else does the impact of management rest so heavily as upon the apparently normal, everyday, bits and pieces of 'to and fro' in the organization.

Some of the issues discussed in this chapter are also considered more fully in other books in this series, specifically entitled, *Client Assessment* by Palmer and McMahon (1997) and *Medical and Psychiatric Issues for Counsellors* by Daines et al. (1997). We have chosen to keep these aspects in this chapter, despite the specialist references just given, because of the management implications of the processes described.

Reception and Threshold Activities

The daily activities of a counselling organization are directly related to its 'threshold activities' (advertising, receiving and contracting with clients). Counselling services having unfriendly and cold reception arrangements may not get too many clients referred! Overly public, indiscreet or too noisy reception areas will be off-putting. And so on.

Adrian McLean posits a series of questions that employees might use to gain a fresh perspective on their own organization. He presents them as follows:

Viewing your Organization as if you were a Visitor from a Foreign Land
Everyday life always looks different when viewed from the outside. To gain a fresh perspective on your organization (eg. your place of work, your university, a social group), think about the following questions:
On first joining   What struck you as being novel, strange or different about the way things happened compared to your expectations or what you had become used to elsewhere?
Think of another organization with which you are familiar   What do you consider to be odd, novel or interesting about the way in which they do things that would be inconceivable in your present organization? What does this say about 'normal' practice in your organization?
That's absolutely typical of us!   If you wanted to convey the essence of how things are done in your organization, capturing both the good and the bad, can you think of a recent event or happening that seems to sum things up? What would it illustrate to an outsider who wanted to learn about your organization?
Heroes, villains and fools!   Think about some of the stories circulating in your organization. What behaviours or character traits lead people to be considered heroes, villains or fools? What messages do they communicate?
On returning to your organization from a new management course.
Imagine that you find a new assignment waiting for you that is tailor-made for the new ideas and skills that you've learned. You're the only member of your organization possessing these skills. What would you expect to happen as you try to implement your new ideas and approaches? What would you need to attend to in order to sustain your initiative, and what people or events would be key in determining its fate? What does this tell you about the character of your organization?
How others see you   What do people from other organizations say about your organization? What do they remark on when they come to

visit, and what overheard or reported comments have you picked up? (McLean, quoted in Morgan, 1989: 32-3)

Reception staff have a very critical role to fulfil within counselling organizations. Sadly, in many 'status-conscious' organizations, receptionists occupy a role of perceived low status and low pay that is in sharp contrast to their value as front-of-house personnel. It is vitally important for the reception staff to embody and reflect the working procedures and principles enshrined in the agency's overall statement of aims and objectives.

Clients and referral agents need to: be welcomed across the threshold; be looked after well through the provision of clear and open information; be located comfortably and discreetly in a waiting area upon arrival; feel able to ask questions of the process they are about to become involved in; and feel that the receptionist takes them seriously and treats them respectfully and compassionately, etc. Inevitably, clients will infer from the ways they have been treated by the reception staff, a wider range of perceptions applicable to the counsellor they end up seeing, the counselling process that ensues, their view of the organization and so on.

Feedback to the authors, from clients, reveals an extraordinary range of attributions and projections emanating from their early contacts with the agency. Clients have variously recorded that their *most critical incident in their therapy* was (a) being invited to have a cup of tea upon arrival, (b) being received warmly and non-intrusively, and (c) being asked reception questions sensitively. These unique, apparently idiosyncratic findings are important for all those engaged in the provision of counselling, particularly managers. They reveal that, sometimes, the important therapeutic work happens not so much within the individual counselling process but rather within the wider context of the organization.

The whole organization has thus to be therapeutic in intention and practice, not just the counsellors. The implications of this statement, in practice, are considerable and are, in substantial part, determined by the overall management system.

Various dimensions of the initial client–organization interface may now be conceptualized.

Clarity of Availability and Punctuality of Opening Hours
This seems an insultingly obvious statement to make. Any agency offering a service to the public needs to advertise its availability,

when it is open, how enquiries can be made, etc. Having advertised them, the agency, except under the most unusual circumstances, needs to observe them. From this matching of advertised and actual agency behaviour, clients and referrers will attribute concepts such as professionalism and dependability upon the organization. The authors have come across agency examples that contradict this basic working premise and as such, these agencies have directly let down their own potential clients, and by inference also let down the wider counselling/psychotherapy profession.

Use of Prior Advertising and Explanatory Leaflets
These will serve the function of offering clients and referrers important preliminary information on the service, such as: what it is set up to do; how to make an appointment; what will happen when contact is established; what is counselling/psychotherapy; can clients choose the gender, culture or race of their counsellor; if a waiting list is used; is the agency equipped to deal with wheelchair access; could it see hearing-impaired clients; what the process of assessment (if any) entails; details of charges; and the nature of confidentiality.

Ensuring Consistency between the Advertising and the Practice
This is somewhat covered in point one above, but also includes the use of answerphone messages, telephone manner, receptionist practices, the maintenance of confidentiality, promptness of response, etc.! Some agencies, eg. one Employee Assistance Programme (EAP), has a policy that its phone should always be answered within a certain number of rings and clients should normally get a first appointment within 3–7 days.

Systems for Putting Clients 'On Hold'
Many organizations may occasionally be oversubscribed by clients. Counselling services employ a variety of mechanisms that include:

- waiting lists
- initial/assessment interviews
- short-term counselling contracts (Culley and Wright, 1997), supportive literature (eg. 'What to do if a counsellor is not immediately available', Sheffield University Counselling Service, 1997)

- relevant texts which can be sent or picked up from the service
- details of other relevant agencies the client may use, etc. (See also the later section on waiting lists.)

Confirmation of Appointments

In circumstances where a client has to wait for an appointment, a supportive letter explaining the situation and confirming the appointment can be very helpful. Nevertheless, this procedure does require careful and sensitive implementation. Receptionists will need to check with each client the appropriateness of and permission to send a letter of confirmation to them or telephone them. Often, clients might reasonably fear that their mail will be opened or their telephone conversations overheard. Protecting client confidentiality, even before they have been seen by a counsellor, is of crucial importance.

Recording Client Details

The above point illustrates some of the subtleties of the reception process. To what extent does the agency consider that it needs particular client details and for what purpose? In circumstances where such details are collected, how are they to be used? For statistics? For understanding patterns of usage? For contacting a client in an emergency (eg. a counsellor being ill, for contacting the client's doctor)?

Subject to the organization's policies, receptionists can reassure clients over these matters by explaining the following:

(a)   that the client can withhold their permission to be contacted, indeed can withhold their personal details

(b)   should the person be written to, the envelope will be a plain one, have no external references as to where it originates, and will be marked Personal and Confidential

(c)   some agencies might also have a printed message on the envelope to allow for the person having moved away, eg. 'If the person is no longer at this address please return this letter to PO Box . . .'. This mechanism is particularly useful with mobile populations, eg. students, but demands that the agency does make special postal arrangements to maintain discretion

(d)   In the event of a telephone call being answered by anyone other than the client, then a simple enquiry will be made, 'Is . . . there please?', 'I am afraid 'so and so' is not here'. In response to the next question, 'who is that speaking?' or 'do you want to leave a message?', the receptionist may just leave a (previously agreed) name for the message to be delivered to the client, eg. 'could you please tell him Janet rang' or may decline and ring off. Some useful pointers on the use of the phone are made in Rosenfield (1997).

(Please note the items above are specific examples derived from one agency – other agencies may develop quite different responses.)

Postal or telephone contact with clients for purposes such as follow-up appointments, surveys and research questionnaires, will all have to be considered carefully within the context of the client–organization relationship. Handled badly, such apparently simple administrative arrangements have the capacity to completely undermine the ethical, confidential relationship the service has with each client.

Are Further Details Required?

Some agencies, either through their receptionist arrangements or later, through the counsellor involved, also collect data such as:

(a)   name and address of client's doctor/surgery
(b)   name and address of next of kin/good friend
(c)   any significant medical condition that it would be important for the counsellor to know about.

In the event that such information as the above is requested (and this assumes that these issues have been fully discussed and decided upon by the management team), the client must be fully reassured that only in the most serious of circumstances would significant others ever be contacted, and then only, if this was at all possible, after they had been informed of this intention.

Some agencies also collect data on client origin, eg. ethnic monitoring or academic department (in the case of students) or employer (in case of employees). This data, once compiled, may be used to review patterns of overall agency usage to inform referring agents or funding bodies.

Waiting Lists

Reference has already been made above to having clients 'on hold', on a waiting list. Waiting lists can prove an enormous anxiety to those responsible for managing an agency. The worst sense can be that of living with a time-bomb waiting to go off. The worries extend from a fear that the as yet unseen client's social, psychological, familial, emotional condition will deteriorate rapidly to the extreme of a waiting client committing suicide.

Colleagues in psychiatric clinics, clinical psychology departments of the NHS and psychotherapy units have had to bear the burden of long waiting lists for many years now. Only in more recent times have counselling and psychotherapy services moved into similar terrain. A variety of coping and holding mechanisms have been evolved over time by different agencies and include the following:

Psychological Boundaries
This perspective is probably best exemplified by a dramatic story shared with one of the authors many years ago by Dr Bernard Ratigan.

> An American volunteer nurse was flown out on a famine relief project by an international aid organization. Within three weeks, sadly, the nurse had a breakdown and had to be flown home. The emerging hypothesis from observers of this experience was that the nurse had neither been helped to find, nor had found within herself, successful psychological mechanisms of managing such enormity of human need with a poverty of resources. There were children, who with food would survive and eventually thrive. There were others, who with food, might pull through. Finally, there were those who could not be saved, however willing the helper and plentiful the food.

Any helper, it is suggested, and perhaps more significantly from the perspective of this book, any manager, will, in times of high demand, have to find both clinical and psychological ways of deciding which clients are seen, when, and in what order . . . and indeed if some are not seen. A triage system for prioritizing work may assist in containing managers' anxieties.

Compilation of Waiting Lists
These may be compiled in a variety of ways. A straight sequential list may be used, recording date of referral/request to be seen,

name, contact address and telephone number, and subsequently the date allocated and to which counsellor, eg.:

Request date	Allocated date	Name	Address	Tel	Couns.
1.3.97	17.3.97	Ann Jones	1 Jones Sq.	123456	DK
2.3.97	17.3.97	Barry Smith	2 Smith St.	234567	CL

More sophisticated systems might record if waiting clients have been offered and then taken up the offer of an assessment/ exploratory interview (discussed later); have been sent a support-ive letter (see below); have indicated their particular concerns and could therefore be sent relevant supportive literature; have been offered other options, eg. group work.

An example of a 'holding' letter used by one student counselling service is given below. Supplementary information is also sent with this letter and comprises a list of other possible supportive contacts in the organization and local area and details of this service's own group work programme.

Dear _____

Appointments with the Counselling Service

We are sorry we are/were unable to offer you an immediate appoint-ment with the service.

Information cards are enclosed with this letter which may inform and assist your present situation by providing a list of other possible contacts for you.

A team of full-time and part-time chaplains is also available in the University. They may be contacted on 2228923 (lunchtimes only).

We will phone or write to you as soon as an appointment becomes available.

I hope we will be able to contact you soon.

Yours sincerely,

Some agencies try to work within a model that responds to particularly acute or urgent situations, as defined by their referring agents or clients themselves. A system of differentiation has therefore to be devised, indicating levels of urgency and possibly specifying those counsellors most suited to the particular circum-stances. Some agencies offer emergency or drop-in slots where the client is the sole determinant of what is urgent. Sometimes an agency devises a secondary waiting list containing those who have been seen for a one-off assessment/exploratory interview and who then go on to wait for counselling.

Assessment and Exploratory Interviews

A one-off interview, offered to clients who are waiting, until such time as they can be seen regularly, is a mechanism that has enabled some agencies to reduce their anxiety levels through knowing, a little more, who is waiting to be seen and what issues are affecting them. The form such preliminary interviews take is very much determined by the theoretical and organizational constraints of the organization and the relative and diagnostic skills of the personnel involved.

Some of the parameters of these primary interviews are specified below.

(a) Is the person who conducts the initial session the same person who will do the counselling later? This factor is an extremely important issue in therapeutic delivery. Successful therapeutic outcomes have been widely understood to have occurred through the relationship, between client and therapists. The initial interview can be more conveniently conceptualized as the basis of an initial meeting and thus start of relationship between the two, if they are to meet again later for counselling. In these circumstances clients may feel relieved that, having begun to tell their story, they will not have to repeat it to a new counsellor, once they 'start counselling'. The counsellor also does not have to guard against too much early bonding between themselves and the client (see the later section on bonding). This first example might best be described as an initial interview.

A second example is that some counselling organizations have used the term 'exploratory' interviews where the client and the counsellor may not meet again after the first session. The term 'exploratory' has been used deliberately, to delineate it from a rather more formal assessment and diagnostic process. Where exploratory or initial interviews have been employed, the time allocated to these may only be 20 minutes to half an hour, though of course can extend up to an hour or more.

Those agencies concerned with offering assessment and diagnostic interviews often have a smaller team of experienced workers who regularly conduct primary interviews. Depending on the nature of assessment and diagnosis, these interviews may last up to an hour and a half.

(b) Primary interviews as an information process Whatever category of interview (outlined above) is employed, one central purpose for the interviewer is that of introducing the client to and explaining the system the agency uses and what the likely steps are, from the waiting list to being seen regularly. To this information may be added other dimensions including the agency's view on confidentiality and ethics, what might happen during the therapeutic process and any additional information that the client seeks.

(c) Therapeutic bonding – to the organization or to the therapist? This aspect seems to be of critical importance to those counselling agencies where the counsellor in the first interview does not go on to become the counsellor later. The difficult task faced by the primary counsellor is facilitating the client's sense of bonding to the organization as a whole rather than to the person of the counsellor. The hope is that if this is successfully achieved, clients will have sufficient trust embedded in the system of the organization that will enable them to move on to the new counsellor and counselling process when that becomes available.

This process of client transition can be very challenging to counselling personnel who are more regularly providing ongoing counselling and then, from time to time, having to conduct these 'one-off' preliminary interviews.

Skills and techniques for maintaining this balance of bonding to the organization (that are different in emphasis to counselling and psychotherapy) include:

 (i)   the provision of more basic information
 (ii) the active use of questions
 (iii) reduced usage of accepting and empathic statements
 (iv) the more systematic gathering of information
 (v)   greater structure and formality.

(d) Assessment of urgency This aspect will in substantial part be tied in to the process of diagnosis and assessment, which is discussed next. The primary counsellor may, in the light of information gathered during the session, wish to recommend to

the agency that this client is offered an earlier set of counselling interviews. There are various research studies that:

(i)   indicate that for some clients promptness in being seen is a crucial factor
(ii) confirm there are different help-seeking trends in clients
(iii) have explored client reasons for non-attendance or single attendance, etc. (Howe, 1993; Oldfield, 1983).

There are considerable differences, inevitably, between different primary counsellors and how they assess urgency. Managers, therefore, may have to maintain an overview of the system of diagnostic interviews in order to monitor the differing emphases of judgement being ascribed by the different primary counsellors.

(e) Other options   Some organizations promote other forms of support and intervention in addition to the supply of individual counselling. After the preliminary session the primary counsellor might consider the client could be helped by other therapeutic activities (until the individual counselling can start and replace or add to them). Within this sphere, both in- and out-house facilities can be considered: eg. support groups, focused workshops, relaxation sessions, yoga.

Assessment and Diagnosis

Reference has already been made, in this chapter, to another book in this series, *Client Assessment*, by Palmer and McMahon (1997). The theoretical, practical and technical aspects of assessment and diagnosis are thus explored in more substantial detail there.

'Assessment literally means to "sit by" ', asserts Ruddell, the author of the first chapter in the above-mentioned book. He suggests that this literal meaning is most important to hold in mind when faced with the prospect of eliciting information from a client (p. 7). He goes on to posit various benefits, purposes and methods used in the assessment and diagnostic processes. Later chapters in the same book also consider client history taking, associated administration, psychiatric assessment and selecting appropriate forms of therapeutic intervention. Approached from the perspective of agency management, these processes can be seen to present a formidable challenge. This is indicated by the following points.

- From a theoretical and philosophical perspective, is the agency or are all the counsellors satisfied with incorporating the assessment process into their work?
- Are all the counsellors to be involved in assessment and diagnosis?
- If only some are, how will they be selected?
- What systems for assessment and diagnosis will be chosen by the organization and are these consistent with the (range of) therapeutic practice offered?
- Will training be offered to the assessors?
- Will the assessment process include client–counsellor matching and allocation?
- How will consistency of practice be monitored and maintained?
- What processes could be introduced to assess the value of these procedures, as perceived by clients and by counsellors?

Payment of Client Fees

Of the three major taboo subjects of our era – sex, death and money – money is the least likely to be spoken about by analysts . . . As James Hillman (1982) remarks: 'patients more readily reveal what's concealed by their pants than what's hidden in their pants' pocket.' . . . As long ago as 1913, Freud commented: 'Money matters are treated by civilized people in the same way as sexual matters, with the same inconsistency, prudishness and hypocrisy' (Freud, 1913). . . . In our paper, we wish to go abroad and explore the world of money, and why it is that clinicians seen to be resistant to thinking and talking about money'. (Haynes and Wiener, 1996)

The quote immediately above, from an article by two analytic therapists, points us to the very considerable difficulties that potentially exist in the nature of the financial relationship between the client and the counselling organization. The authors note that many training organizations fail to provide the conditions in which their members and trainees can reflect upon their money complexes (1996: 16). They also note that, historically, analysts have neglected their conscious and unconscious feelings about money. In this regard we would assert that analysts are only reflecting the cultural complexities that are deeply embedded in our society (and perhaps western societies in general) associated with money.

Appleyard (1993) notes that money, like time, was only, originally, an artificial concept that society has concretized over many centuries. Now its existence is viewed as absolute, a solid and substantive phenomenon, around which society functions; and of this view there are very few doubters! Appleyard discusses the complex intertwining of older, traditional belief systems and how money has come to constitute such a meaning system itself in contemporary life. Philosophic and spiritual beliefs have, for many, been overtaken by systems of meaning attributed to the apparently concrete symbol of money!

Zeldin (1994) also charts the complex relationship of British culture to money in his *An Intimate History of Humanity*. Quoting from a wide range of sources, he offers the following comments:

> Their god (the merchants), Hermes, was a trickster and a thief. Plato laid it down that it was impossible to engage in trade and be virtuous at the same time, though his academy was funded by a merchant. St. Thomas Aquinas said merchants were bound to have trouble attaining salvation, because the temptation to sin was inherent in their occupation . . . When Napoleon called the English a nation of shopkeepers it was like calling them a nation of pimps. (Zeldin, 1994: 154-5)

In rounding off this all too brief introduction to this section, let us return again to the article by Haynes and Wiener.

> During a series of meetings to discuss our clinical work, we came to two shared realizations. Firstly, we agreed that money has exceptional status in the analytic setting. Although, for our patients, the transference meanings of money are very important, the fact remains that our patients pay us: an actual exchange of money does take place. We cannot think of another example of a sustained concrete exchange in the therapeutic relationship . . . Secondly, we discovered that neither of us are at ease with our own attitudes and behaviour in relation to money. Money itself is a technical means of exchange which allows certain transactions and professional relationships to take place. As such it is neutral with no second nature; there is nothing powerful about it. However, all analysts know that money is extremely powerful and we live in a society where money has great importance as it bestows security, status and power. Tom Wolfe has described the spirit of the 1990s as that of 'money fever' and the introduction of a National Lottery has re-evolved the energy of a collective delusional fantasy of the tantalizing crock of gold at the end of the rainbow. (Haynes and Wiener, 1996: 15)

All of the above points us to the enormous complexities underpinning the exchange of money for therapy. The tension between altruism and greed, and the relationship between soul and money are beset with contradictory arguments confronting each therapist. The therapist's (and agencies') dependency upon client income is also inherent in the financial transaction and constitutes a shadow dimension that few care to recognize.

These issues will, of course, impact differently upon different therapists and different agencies. Independent practitioners, precisely because they operate in individual circumstances without even receptionist support, will have to confront these issues in everyday practice with clients. Only they can transact with the client. Only they can decide upon fee levels, sliding scales, methods of payment, systems of dealing with non-payment of fees, etc.

For some agencies, eg. some employee assistance schemes, college-based counselling services and some voluntary organizations, this issue does not have to be dealt with as the funding basis for the work originates elsewhere and not from the client. Beyond this, however, a huge range of counselling and psychotherapy organizations do have to deal with this issue on a daily basis.

Administration and Practicalities of Client Finance
At least five particular areas of practice require organizational attention in this regard.

1. (a) Who informs the client of the fee(s) expected? (Information)
   (b) Who negotiates the fee if there is a sliding structure? (Negotiation)
2. How are the decisions of fee level recorded? (Contracting)
3. (a) Who collects the fee(s)? (Collection)
   (b) What are the systems of payment? (Administration)
4. What happens in the event of session cancellation? (Cancellation)
5. What processes exist that deal with clients' dissatisfaction with services rendered? (Dissatisfaction).

Information   Information on client fees may simply be provided, initially, through information leaflets on the agency, and further substantiated by reception staff or counsellor upon enquiry.

Decisions as to fee levels, the existence and range of sliding scales and the possibility of free sessions are, of course, subsumed under management responsibility. Initially, then, in a service having fixed fees, or indeed a fee range, the receptionist will primarily be informing the client of the agency's advertised practices.

Negotiation This secondary level, of negotiating fees consonant with the client's capacity to pay and the agency's need to ensure sufficient funding has much more complexity attached to it. Our contention is that any negotiation of fees with clients ought really to take place with the therapist, within the initial session, in the therapy room. Negotiations over financial matters as we have alluded to in the introduction are deemed to be private within our culture and not for public consumption. For example, what feelings would you experience if asked, publicly, about the size of your salary or if the bank teller announced in a voice loud enough for other customers to hear, following your enquiry, the present state of your bank account? The extent, or not, of a client's income and the feelings and meanings the client attaches to this aspect of their lives are profoundly personal. In addition, the very issue of finance may be part of the client's difficulties over which they have sought help.

Extraordinary skill and sensitivity are required by therapists in conducting such delicate negotiations and arriving at a mutually agreeable position. Where issues of money are related to the client's concerns, or their self-esteem, or their political view of the world, then therapists not only have to conduct the initial financial negotiation (that embodies real, material, financial exchange) but have to remain open to continued dialogues where the client may disagree with earlier decisions reached and disparage the worthwhileness of the counselling they are receiving.

Contracting In all circumstances that we are aware of, a verbal agreement reached between the client and counsellor acts as the operational basis for their later work together. In circumstances where the receptionist collects the fees, a mechanism obviously has to exist so that he or she is informed of the exact amount agreed. This could be achieved through verbal means, where the counsellor informs the receptionist after the interview, or through written means, possibly as one aspect of an initial interview form containing basic client details and held at reception.

Where modifications to the agreed fee are requested by clients, we would suggest that this is conducted within the therapy process. Receptionists will need to know of this policy and, importantly, understand its rationale. From an analytic perspective the reader may appreciate the potential for splitting that is inherent in this particular arena. The client could easily play the receptionist off against the therapist.

Such dynamics are inevitable and certainly worthy of recognition and therapeutic consideration (depending on the theoretical basis of the work) within the counselling sessions. Nevertheless, an operational clarity is required so that receptionists are not placed in awkward situations. Enough other arenas of potential difficulty can exist in the receptionist–client–therapist relationship for this to be added to it! Inevitably there won't *always* be negotiations involved. Indeed, some communicative psychotherapists consider that such third parties always have the potential to violate the therapeutic frame (Gray, 1994; Smith, 1991).

The above considerations point yet again to the importance of regular communications occurring between reception and counselling staff on both informal and formal levels (eg. staff meetings).

Collecting Clarity of process is urged throughout this section. An agency might decide, because of its particular circumstances, that the receptionist might be a more appropriate person than the counsellor to collect the fees or vice versa. That the process is made clear to the client and is clear to staff seems vitally important.

Administration and cancellation Methods of payment are a further aspect that will need to have been clarified in the initial negotiation. Where cash is an acceptable form the nominated collector (receptionist or therapist) must have access to sufficient change through the provision of a regular 'float' perhaps on a daily basis, or sessional basis, if different staff work at different times of the day. The use of cheques may prove most convenient and demand that they are cursorily inspected for inaccurate or incorrect completion, thus saving time, inconvenience and delays of payment, where mistakes are picked up by the agency's bank. It is not impossible that some organizations might even offer credit card facilities for payment, though the authors don't know of any such examples.

A policy also has to be considered in relation to:

(a) the possibility of payments made on a sessional basis
(b) payments being made retrospectively for a series of sessions
(c) the payment of a fee for the preliminary session
(d) the projected fee for the number of agreed sessions before therapy has started
(e) what fee payment is required in relation to a cancellation of a session by the client.

Some organizations divide this particular aspect in such a way as to allow for length of notice of warning that has been given that a client may not be able to turn up. The organization may be able to save paying for the therapist's time if it knows early enough that the client is not able to turn up. As with so many other subjects in this book, this particular facet is also interrelated and interwoven with many of the other areas of organization of the service. Specific to the above, both the financial basis of the organization as well as the contracts of employment for the counsellors are implicated.

An appropriate procedure for the issue of receipts for fees received is also required.

Dissatisfaction We have included this section with some un-certainty and anxiety. We have wondered about the particular implications arising from a client's expressed dissatisfaction with the therapy received and the possible demand for their money back!

Different sales organizations have procedures for reimbursing shoppers, for example, if the goods are deemed damaged or shoddy in any way. As we understand it, the purchaser is pro-tected by law, to some extent, in seeking financial redress for being sold items that are not satisfactory. By contrast, in the human services area (eg. health, physiotherapy, dentistry) what facilities exist for clients of such services to seek some element of financial redress for 'unsatisfactory' therapy? This issue of money, of course, will raise many aspects of and for therapeutic work, as Haynes and Weiner (1996) have pointed out so clearly. Notwith-standing the theoretical issues, clients may feel fully justified in requesting their money back or seeking a reduction in fees following therapy that they have judged as inadequate, for whatever reason. They could, of course, seek legal advice and intervention, ultimately seeking compensation.

What is it that their fees have bought? Therapist time? Therapist's care? Promises of behaviour change? Reductions in stress and anxiety levels? Increases in confidence? Freedom from a phobia?

We are not sufficiently informed to advise readers on this rather grey area of professional practice. We certainly would encourage organizations to be very explicit about what they offer, what they can and cannot deliver and what the fee payment covers. In this way they will be offering an explicit contract to each client that will be (at worst) defensible in court should it come to that (Jenkins, 1997).

Complaints Procedures

This particular aspect, of course, raises the wider issue of complaints policies and procedures that an agency might adopt or construct. A sample complaints document is featured in the Appendix and the subject is further dealt with in Chapter 7.

Case Notes and Agency Records: Confidentiality and Appropriateness

A previous section in this chapter has already discussed the recording of client details by reception staff. Two major questions were raised there: what is recorded and why? The recording of case notes is a necessary and standard part of professional practice for counsellors. Two further questions now emerge. How are case notes recorded and where are they kept?

Different practices inevitably exist in different agencies. The question as to the location of the records and notes can be somewhat determined by the nature of the organization. Consider, for example, an employee assistance scheme that operates administratively from a central bureau but has counsellors in various locations around the country. A referral comes into the agency and basic client details are taken. Arrangements are then made by the receptionist for the client to be seen by a counsellor in that counsellor's location, which could be many miles away from the administrative base of the service. How are the original details communicated to the counsellor? By phone? By letter/standard form? By fax or e-mail?

What is communicated? Name? Address? Gender? Employer? Referring agent, if different from employer? Nature of presenting difficulty? Details of Dr?, etc. Does the receptionist keep one copy for the central records?

In turn, what are the expectations on the counsellor for the secure storage of these records and the case notes? Does the central agency, after the completion of therapy, expect a copy of the case notes for its own records or does it require just a brief synopsis of the work after counselling has finished?

Counsellors in Germany also have to submit accounts of their therapeutic work with clients to assessors employed by health insurance companies who recommend (or not) that the therapist is paid. 'Managed care' systems in the USA also require particular practices antithetical to most contemporary professional practice in Britain. These particular examples, whilst not presently or directly applicable to the British situation, could emerge in future years within the UK. Huge question marks abound in these circumstances as to the nature of client confidentiality, the externally perceived worthwhileness of the counsellors' work, retrospective payments and so on. Also, because case records, in this instance, are not kept within the confines of the organizational setting, the risk of breaches of confidentiality occurring are increased substantially. British equivalents in this regard might include employers requesting details of an employee's therapy where the employer has paid the bill.

Different patterns of practice inevitably emerge for different organizations. Perhaps what is most important here is the centrality of concern the agency retains in ensuring the right balance between the maintenance of appropriate confidentiality for clients with the agency's need for information. If all case records are held centrally by the agency who else has access to them? How secure are they? If the agency retains the core statistical data and the therapists keep their own case records, is there clear delineation of which is kept where? Also do the therapists have access to secure storage facilities of their own?

Monitoring of Boundaries: Loose Talk and Confidentiality

Many aspects of this book are concerned with the very appropriate, formal structures and systems that are required by any professional counselling agency. Some of the challenges to the management of such agencies may nevertheless come from the rather less formal, interpersonal behaviours and dynamics of the staff team. One particular aspect of concern, for example, will be how standards of professional demeanour and discretion can be maintained when colleagues may be stressed, either themselves or about clients. Loose talk by staff in reception areas and staff rooms can have considerably negative effects upon clients waiting in an adjacent room. Often, when counsellors are working with a particularly difficult client they may want to 'sound off' their concerns, after the session, with a colleague or the receptionist. This can so easily be done in the heat of the moment, in complete contradiction to the professional aspirations of each of the complainers. The human need to sound off can temporarily overcome the general limits of professional demeanour that therapists operate within.

In this sense, secretaries and receptionists in counselling services can be placed in extremely difficult and stressful circumstances. Though the counsellor may rationalize this process as 'sounding off' or stress reducing, the effect upon the secretary could also be considerable and pressurizing. Is the secretary personally and professionally equipped to listen to these brief stories? Do they feel that an expectation is on them to be wise, to offer case supervision, to emotionally support the counsellor, to suspend what they are doing for the moment?

Two main issues, therefore, emerge from the phenomenon of 'loose talk'. The first is that of the continuing maintenance of a professionally discreet atmosphere that ensures that all users of the service do not inadvertently hear things that they should not. The second issue refers to the considerable pressure that reception and secretarial staff can be put under. Counsellors can often forget that the receptionist (who may well be a very pleasant reception person) may not be trained as a counsellor and therefore may not understand the counsellor concerns, may not know what to say in response, may wonder why the counsellor is not speaking to their supervisor about this and finally, might experience considerable stress in knowing about a client's difficulties.

Who supervises the secretary? Who supports the secretary? The manager has to pay attention to this particular staff need also.

Referrals to and Relationships with Other Agencies

From time to time, particular circumstances will demand that a client may need to be referred to further specialist help. In addition, where counselling agencies operate within particular organizational or community settings, clients may need to be referred in to the agency. The process of successful referral can require considerable skill and sensitivity.

Counselling agencies may often be perceived in particular ways by referrers, some of which may be quite inaccurate and unrealistic. Further, some referrers may be only too glad to 'dump' the referred client upon the counselling agency, thus successfully avoiding, possibly, their particular responsibilities in relation to the client, eg. some alcohol counselling agencies seem to be used as dumping grounds for any difficult client who mentions a drink problem. A related problem is that many specialist agencies often find they are doing generalist counselling (or eg. sexual abuse) once clients have gone beyond the presenting problem (eg. drink) stage.

A very helpful booklet on making referrals was produced by Liverpool University Counselling Service some years ago. A set of referral guidelines and checklist from this document are detailed below.

Referral Guidelines and Checklist

1. Know the community resources for different kinds of services.
2. Explore the client's readiness for referral.
3. Be direct and honest about your observation of their behaviour that led to your suggested referral. Be honest about your own limitations.
4. It is usually desirable to discuss the possibility of referral with the referral agency before the problem becomes urgent.
5. Determine which other persons have had contact with this client and confer with them before suggesting further steps, bearing in mind, however, the constraints of confidentiality.
6. Be fair in explaining the services of a referral agency by citing the possibilities and the limitations of that agency. Do not imply that miracles can be performed there.

7. Do not release information to any referral sources without permission from clients.
8. If you have the primary helping relationship with the client, it is ethical to maintain that relationship until the referral is complete and a new relationship is begun.

In the case of counselling services working within a large organizational setting, the publication of a similar advisory document for distribution to the key people in the referring organization might prove of immense benefit.

Management of Accounts and Salaries

This might be a particular arena that many counsellors may not be familiar with until elevated to a managerial role. The appropriate maintenance and management of the financial side of organizations, including the pay-roll of employees has considerable demands as a task in itself. There is a range of legal responsibilities that have to be fulfilled in this regard and managers, depending on their previous experience, would be well advised to employ, even on a part-time basis, an appropriately qualified person to both advise and carry out the financial tasks.

The prompt, regular and correct payment of staff, with due regard to salary scales, tax payments, national insurance, honoraria, expenses, etc. is an important facet of any organization. The impact of late or incorrect payments on staff morale can be considerable and, particularly in counselling, where there is already stress and duress, any inadvertent payment errors may cause huge emotional reactions. Not all counsellors are paid salaries, a situation which is determined by the organization being worked in. Even so, the prompt payment of honoraria and expenses to such staff can carry a strong symbolic significance to those particular individuals.

The overall financial situation of the organization requires regular monitoring through the efficient maintenance of accounts. This statement, of course, is based upon the law of the land as it relates both to organizations and taxation (eg. VAT) as well as more general business sense.

Charitable and voluntary organizations will normally have systems in place for the annual, if not more regular, presentation of accounts to their governing bodies. Accounts, of course, also require formal auditing and formal acceptance.

Bearing in mind the very wide range of counselling organizations (eg. charitable trusts, voluntary organizations, partnerships, co-operatives, limited companies) this section is necessarily brief as it would require too much detail to cover all of these situations, but it is included to underline the extremely important element of organizational structure. The implications of not taking this seriously are only too obvious, including the foreclosure of the agency, letting clients down, and at worst, bankruptcy and litigation.

Key Points

- The systems and conventions of various daily working practices require regular attention by managers.
- Review your agency's reception arrangements as they relate to clients.
- Advertise and keep opening hours punctual.
- Clients and referral agents can be orientated to the service by good information leaflets.
- Review regularly the agency's system for waiting list management.
- What records of clients are really needed and collected?
- The issues of assessment and diagnosis need to be considered.
- Establish clear systems for negotiation and collection of client fees.
- Consider the implementation of a complaints procedure.
- What records are kept and where?
- Avoid loose talk around the office.
- Alert other agencies and your own staff to the skills of referral.
- Ensure the financial side of the organization is efficient, well administered and regularly audited.
- Try not to pay staff late!

6

Managing Crisis

This chapter is about managing crisis. There are five distinct topics that are covered. The first features the systems and processes that need to be in place to help individual clients in crisis. The second topic covers the systems and processes needed to help the counselling agency cope with the consequences for the agency of crises. The third topic details the need for a counselling service working within an organization to have contingency plans for a crisis within that organization; for example, major redundancies, death in a department, fatal industrial accidents, death in a student flat, a shooting incident within a police force and so on. Fourthly we have written very briefly about responding to a crisis by setting up a telephone helpline. Finally there is a paragraph about the possible impact of the electronic revolution – the Internet and electronic mail – on counselling organizations.

Managing Clients' Crises

A general issue that all counselling organizations need to resolve as a matter of policy is whether they offer a 24-hour emergency service. If the decision is that they do not offer a 24-hour service then they may want to offer information to out-of-hours callers about their opening hours and alternative sources of help and support during the hours that they are closed. This information, if it is decided as a matter of policy to provide it, will need to be available on the telephone answering machine, perhaps on the outside door of the agency and in leaflets and literature that the agency makes available to actual and potential clients. Counselling agencies that are on the Internet may choose to include the information on their home page.

Most agencies will experience clients who have self-referred or have been referred who are in crisis. Such clients may need to see, or speak with, a counsellor as a matter of urgency. And sometimes equally urgently they may need to be referred on for specialist help. Such specialist help may range from accommodation and legal help, through to medical and psychiatric treatment needed as a matter of urgency. This raises a number of issues.

Counselling Appointments for Crisis Clients

How does an agency ensure that crisis clients can be seen either immediately or at very short notice? Different types of organizations manage this in a number of different ways.

During opening hours Sheffield University Counselling Service tries to ensure that at least one counselling session per day is available in an emergency. If a distressed client cannot be seen immediately then a supportive responsibility will fall on the reception staff. Receptionists need to be given training and support to work with distressed clients, not as counsellors but as supporters, until the client can see a counsellor. Such responsibility means that the reception staff must be included in the Service's staff processing meetings. We will suggest later that the reception staff should be in these staff meetings even if they have not had to work with crisis clients. Another means of helping crisis clients used by the above Service is to ensure that in the waiting room there is a range of leaflets, pamphlets and other reading materials that deal with at least some of the referring problems that may have brought the clients to the Service, for example, sexual orientation, drugs, relationships, alcohol and debt. Self-service drinks are also available in the waiting room.

The Samaritans have a local call rate telephone number connected to a system that ensures that if the staff of the local branch are all busy on the telephones, then the call is automatically transferred to the next most local branch, an idea that could be adopted by any telephone helpline organization that has multiple branches.

Clearly those organizations that are set up specifically to deal with crisis clients, such as rape crisis centres, need to try and maintain a level of staffing that ensures that there is always a trained staff member who can work with a client arriving in a distressed condition, or ringing in a distressed condition. As a general policy matter, each counselling organization needs to have a policy and systems in place to cope with crisis clients.

Crisis Referrals

Where emergency referrals to specialists are needed then the agency needs to have those facilities in place. For example, the agency needs to know where the nearest accident and emergency service is situated and its opening hours.

Ideally the agency needs to have an arrangement with a local psychiatrist or the local psychiatric service so that emergency referrals can be made. When we wrote of management committees and steering groups we then commented on the desirability of having a psychiatrist on such bodies to act as a psychiatric advisor to the agency.

In cases where the counsellor has reason to think that a client is a danger to themselves or to others, the client may need to be admitted to a hospital. If they are not prepared to be admitted as a voluntary patient then they may be 'sectioned' under the Mental Health Act (1983) and detained for a period of up to three days or up to four weeks. For a client to be 'sectioned' for three days (Section 4) an Approved Social Worker (approved by the local authority as having special experience of mental illness) or the nearest relative, plus one doctor need to agree. For a four-week 'section' (Section 2) one Approved Social Worker and two doctors, one of whom must be an Approved Doctor (a doctor approved under Section 12 of the Mental Health Act (1983) as having special experience of mental disorders) have to agree. The Act only applies to England and Wales, but Scotland and Northern Ireland have similar legislation. It is clearly good practice for a counselling agency to have the name, address and telephone numbers of Approved Social Workers and Approved Doctors readily available. Even if the client is prepared to be admitted as a voluntary patient the referral will have to be made through a doctor. For a fuller discussion of medical and psychiatric issues for counsellors see Daines et al. (1997).

Part of the client record keeping of an agency should be the client's General Practitioner's name, address and telephone number. This may be important in a crisis. Many counsellors and therapists also keep a record of the client's psychiatric record and their current and past medication. All of this information may be useful in the case of an emergency.

Services may choose, as a matter of policy, to have a car available at all times so that crisis patients may be transported if this is needed, or so that the location of the crisis can be visited if that is more appropriate. As the previous sentence indicates, there may well be circumstances in which a client in crisis needs to be taken somewhere, but this eventuality does demand prior consideration of such issues because of the possible insurance implications.

Managing Agency Crises

By the very nature of counselling the clients come as a result of crises; either they can no longer cope with their life as it is, for them their life has reached a critical point; or, there has been a critical event in their life which has been traumatic and their response has been to seek help and support. In this sense counsellors are always responding to a crisis. When we think of just some of the presenting problems that clients bring to counselling services we can see how counsellors spend their life working with emotive issues and trauma – with crises and people in crisis.

One issue which may arise for counselling agencies' staff is their physical safety. A client may become violent. At Sheffield University Counselling Service this eventuality is guarded against by ensuring that there are always at least two members of staff in the building at any time, and by the provision of panic buttons to summon help in an emergency.

It is well known that emotive work can lead to burnout, and less well known that it can lead to vicarious traumatization. It may also be that the agency, and not just individual counsellors, may become burnt out or vicariously traumatized by the work. A further related problem can be crisis and trauma at one remove. For example, a police officer in a specialist unit dealing with trauma and crisis comes to see the Force counsellor because they have become burnt out or vicariously traumatized by their life of dealing with the victims of rape and rapists, victims of paedophilia and paedophiles, or victims of domestic violence and the domestically violent or the victims of road traffic accidents and the initiators of road traffic accidents. These officers are not traumatized clients but vicariously traumatized clients who may in

their turn cause their counsellor to become burnt out or vicariously traumatized. Nurses, doctors, ambulance crew and fire
officers may be similar clients for their welfare or counselling
services.

Burnout
Burnout can be understood as a process or as a state (Shirom,
1989), but there is general agreement about the impact of emotive
work for workers in the caring professions. Shirom concluded
that the core meaning of burnout is '. . . a combination of physical
fatigue, emotional exhaustion and cognitive weariness'. When we
consider a range of writing on burnout a number of other words
keep recurring in the definitions that are offered – 'detached',
'withdrawal', 'cynicism' (Shirom, 1989).

A counsellor who displays or is beginning to display burnout as
described above is clearly not only paying a heavy personal price
for their work (physical, emotional and cognitive exhaustion) but
is also not going to be in a position to help counselling clients
(detached, withdrawn and cynical).

McCann and Pearlman (1990) report research on burnout
amongst therapists which suggests that factors which lead to
burnout can include professional isolation, the emotional drain of
always being empathic, ambiguous success, lack of therapeutic
success, non-reciprocated giving and attentiveness and failure to
live up to one's own expectations, leading to feelings of inadequacy or incompetence.

Having looked briefly at the causes and symptoms of burnout
we are in a position to look at how an organization can look after
its staff so that the client crises and the nature of the work do not
impact on the staff as individuals and on the ability of the agency
to meet the needs of the clients.

Preventing and Coping with Burnout
Looking at the causes of burnout suggests some ways that the
consequences can be avoided by a counselling organization.
Professional isolation can be addressed through a deliberate effort
towards collegiality; through membership of groups of counsellors who meet regularly where working as a counsellor can be
discussed informally without breaching confidentiality; through
peer supervision, group supervision and individual supervision. It
is certainly this author's experience that being in group super-

vision not only helps combat professional isolation but, through being based on listening to the work, professional difficulties and clinical struggles of colleagues, leads to a sense of shared struggle and success that greatly reduces the sense of professional isolation. This sense can easily set in when you feel you are the only counsellor in the world who is struggling and who arrives at supervision confused and disappointed with the work that you are doing. I owe thanks to my colleagues with whom I have been in group supervision over the years. To help combat the possibility of professional isolation one counselling service has instituted a staff coffee break so that staff can all meet informally together in the midst of their working day. A possible addition for agencies would be to have process meetings that are to deal specifically with the processes of working as a member of the agency – the feelings and experiences that are the work. If such meetings are instituted then great care needs to be taken that administrative and systems matters do not intrude – they are matters for a separate meeting. A multipurpose meeting will certainly not help group process designed to support and help staff in their emotive work. Such process meetings should include all of the staff of the agency, not just the counsellors.

Supervision also helps with the causes of burnout such as failure to live up to one's expectations when these are, or have become, unrealistic. Supervision can be wonderful for getting a counsellor's feet back on the ground and for reality testing their world and professional ambitions. If the supervision is provided by members of the agency there is a danger of keeping problems and pressure within the agency, to the potential long-term disadvantage of the agency. In many circumstances supervision is best provided by supervisors outside the counselling organization.

Burnout can also be caused by excessive workload, and all counselling agencies and individual counsellors should observe the implications of the Codes of Professional Practice that urge that excessive workloads are not undertaken. The BAC suggests that a full caseload is 20 client hours per week. McCann and Pearlman (1990) also suggest that counsellors need variety in their work to avoid being harmed by their counselling work. Thus, as in the BAC Code of Practice, agencies and individuals should ensure a variety of work and professional development, such as including further training, research, writing and teaching.

A counsellor who is in therapy as a client will also find a way of both coping with and preventing burnout by having the opportunity to reflect on their life, ambitions and work and to subsequently make healthy choices about their life. Perhaps the most important aids to coping with burnout are to be aware of it as a condition, know what the causes are and recognize the symptoms: forewarned is forearmed; prevention is better than cure.

Vicarious Traumatization

Working directly or indirectly with victims of trauma can gradually result in a counsellor or therapist becoming vicariously traumatized. This means that the counsellor begins to show symptoms that are characteristic of traumatized people. They may well develop the symptoms of post-traumatic stress disorder (PTSD). In a sense this is a stage beyond burnout, and is different from burnout. It is possible to be burnt out but not be vicariously traumatized and it is possible to be vicariously traumatized without being burnt out, although they often go together. There is considerable overlap of symptoms, as noted by Carroll and White (1982), who list symptoms of burnout and show how they overlap with those of PTSD.

The broad list of symptoms of PTSD are:

■ The traumatic event is persistently re-experienced
■ Persistent avoidance of stimuli associated with the trauma
■ The numbing of general responsiveness
■ Persistent symptoms of increased arousal
■ The duration of the disturbance is more than one month
■ The disturbances cause clinically significant distress or impairment in social, occupational, or other important areas of functioning (Taken from American Psychiatric Association, 1994).

McCann and Pearlman (1990) spell out in more detail how a counsellor or therapist might manifest these symptoms after working with traumatized clients.

Therapists may experience painful images and emotions associated with their client's traumatic memories and may, over time, incorporate these memories into their own memory system. As a result, therapists may find themselves experiencing PTSD symptoms, including intrusive thoughts or images [or smells, or sounds] and painful emotional reactions . . . there is a risk that the helper may feel numb or emotionally distant, thus unable to maintain a warm, empathetic and responsive stance with clients. (1990: 144) (The contents of the brackets are added by this author.)

They go on to argue that therapists' cognitive schema (the way that they make sense of the world and relate to it) may be altered as part of vicarious traumatization. Specifically they write of the deterioration and undermining of beliefs and behaviours around trusting and dependency, safety, power, esteem, intimacy and frame of reference (the element of a client's story that is picked out for attention). They clearly set out the possible impact of working with traumatized clients so that we can see the symptoms of vicarious traumatization and clearly observe the symptoms that a vicariously traumatized counsellor would begin to display. A vicariously traumatized counsellor is not going to be able to work professionally with clients.

Preventing and Coping with Vicarious Traumatization

As with burnout, it is important that counsellors know about vicarious traumatization so that they can keep themselves safe, self-diagnose and seck help if they are suffering. They may also need to stop working with clients, at least for some time whilst they seek help and support. The BAC Code suggests that this would be professional behaviour. Counselling services have a duty of care to ensure that their counsellors are safe, do not overwork and do receive adequate training, support and supervision: a duty to monitor their staff for the sake of the staff and the clients.

What specifically can individual counsellors and their organization do to prevent vicarious traumatization? McCann and Pearlman (1990) suggest the following.

- Strive for balance between personal and professional lives
- Balance the clinical caseload with other professional activities such as teaching and research
- Balance victim and non-victim cases
- Be aware of respecting personal boundaries, such as limiting evening or weekend work
- Develop realistic expectations about counselling victims of trauma
- Allow/encourage the experiencing of full emotional reactions

■ Seek out non-victim related activities that provide hope and optimism
■ In case conferences/supervision share the rewards that are inherent in counselling work.

Gabriel (1994) suggests the following extra strategies.

■ Supervision that emphasizes the intellectual techniques necessary to the work
■ Rotation of duties
■ Stress management
■ Instituting rituals that permit therapists to grieve in a formal acceptable manner for their clients.

Traumatic Incidents within the Agency

We have written so far of the steady accumulation of work pressure within a counselling organization leading to burnout and vicarious traumatization. Now we are going to look at how the organization can manage a crisis within itself that is related to a single incident that effects either a single individual or a number of the staff up to and including the whole of the staff. Such an incident might be a client going berserk within the agency building or a client committing suicide or dying, or the collective immediate work of the counsellors with the victims of a major single traumatic event. The immediate impact of working with those involved with the King's Cross underground station fire might well be an example of traumatized counsellors.

The process that is available to use with such people is called Critical Incident Debriefing (CID) or Psychological Debriefing. Essentially the technique requires that all of the staff who were involved in the incident, however directly or indirectly, are debriefed as a group. Each person in the group is invited by the facilitator(s) to talk through what they did, what they thought and what they felt. There are a number of variations of this technique, but they have more in common than distinguishes them. The process is fully discussed in Meichenbaum (1997). The technique can also be used for a single individual if they alone were subject to a traumatic incident. Some evidence has suggested that if CID is used between two and four days after the incident then the incidence of PTSD is reduced by 80 per cent. However, Meichenbaum suggests that there is little hard research evidence to support the efficacy of CID, and that indeed there is some evidence that suggests that it might be counterproductive unless it is used very carefully and with appropriate follow-up counselling and support.

A counselling organization could provide its own CID for an individually traumatized colleague or sub-group of the agency, but it would be better and more appropriate if colleagues did not act as counsellors for one another and an outside counsellor was brought in to facilitate the CID. There are a number of specialist organizations in CID and many EAP organizations also offer this specialist service.

A Major Crisis within the Parent Organization

Counselling services that are located within an organization in order to serve the staff of that organization need to have plans and resources to cope with a major crisis within that organization. The type of crises that we have in mind are a shooting incident within a police force, a significant industrial accident within an organization, the death of an important staff member or a major closure or redundancy programme.

The counselling organization needs to plan and anticipate such events and consider the probability of them occurring. The agency needs the resources to counsel a number of staff members (which may be quite large in the case of say a major redundancy programme) and they will need the training to be able to mobilize a CID programme if that is the appropriate immediate response.

Not only is there a need to plan the counselling resources for a major emergency, but there is also a need to inform managers and individuals of the services available. There may also be a need to educate individuals and managers about the benefits of counselling and the likelihood of people needing help after emergencies. The culture of some organizations is that people should be able to cope with trauma and stress without any need for support or counselling. This author recently heard a manager refer to staff 'wimping out'. Part of the service for organization-based agencies may well be educational.

Telephone Helplines

The setting up and running of telephone helplines as a response to crises is a large and rapidly growing field and follows on the older practice of telephone support services like the Samaritans and Child Line. The Telephone Helplines Association, founded in 1996, has over 800 organizations as members. These members' lines took over 14 million calls in 1996. The Association is planning to move into the field of emergency helplines in addition to working with long-life helplines. This is such a specialist area of work that organizations intending to set up telephone helplines, or to add them to their range of resources, would be well advised to seek the help of the Telephone Helplines Association. The Samaritans provide specialist training courses for the staff of helpline services and advice.

The Internet

The communications revolution that is rolling at increasing speed makes it increasingly possible for geographically distant individuals to speak together, not only by telephone and letter but also by mobile telephone, fax and e-mail. Vast amounts of material can be made available to clients through the Internet if an organization chooses to have a home page. Any counselling organization with access to the Internet can set up a facility that allows clients to contact them, receive whatever material they choose to access that the organization includes on its home page and be counselled or supported via e-mail. This can be done anonymously if the client wishes. The Samaritans already have this facility in many countries including the UK. This very afternoon this author, an Internet beginner, easily contacted the Samaritans in both the UK and Hong Kong simply by typing in 'Samaritans'. Using the Internet the contact between the counsellor/supporter and client can be a continuous two-way typed meeting, or an asynchronous typed correspondence where there is a significant time gap between sending material and receiving a considered response. A third alternative that is technically possible is to have two computers linked through the Internet with the client and the counsellor/supporter in voice contact with one another through speakers and microphones. This voice contact through Internet is known as VON (Voice on the Net). For some present or future counselling organizations the Internet may be the voice of the future. Agencies wanting to investigate the possibilities of the Internet will find that Young (1998) provides a simple introduction for the 'computer frightened'. Potential users of e-mail should remember that confidentiality cannot be guaranteed. All Internet communications, whether typed or through VON, are at the rate charged for local telephone calls, even if the contact is UK to Australia.

The use of e-mail raises a whole raft of managerial and counselling issues that need to be addressed both in terms of how the service is provided and in terms of the training of e-mail counsellors. It may be that an e-mail counselling 'theory' will have to be developed to cope with topics such as the development of psychological relationships, coping with the losses that occur when the spoken word is replaced with the typed word, the time lapse that is implicit in responding via typed e-mail and the client's projections and transference towards an unseen and unheard counsellor. There are also issues around confidentiality, ethics and the identification of the counsellor. For a fuller discussion of these theoretical, training and management issues see Lago (1996, 1997).

Resources

The Telephone Helplines Association can be contacted at 61 Gray's Inn Rd, London WC1X 8LT. Tel: 0171-242 0555; fax: 0171-242 0699; e-mail: 101342.3246@compuserve.com; and web site: http://www.poin2.co.uk./clients/tha/index.htm

The Samaritans can be contacted at 10 The Grove, Slough SL1 1QP. Tel: 01753 532713; fax: 01753 819004; e-mail: jo@samaritans.org or samaritans@anon.penet.fi (the latter e-mail address assures client anonymity).

Registering Your Organization

The United Kingdom Register of Counsellors has schemes for both the registration of individual therapists as well as for organizations which can apply to become a 'Registered Sponsoring Organization'. Further details of the registration scheme may be obtained by contacting the Register Office at the British Association for Counselling. Tel: 01788 568739. The Association for University and College Counselling is also piloting a scheme for student counselling services, and enquiries may be made to AUCC via the BAC offices.

7

Managing Managing!

Managing leadership in large corporations is . . . facing complex issues that require not only decisiveness but creativity: not only managerial control but visionary leadership; not only the technical skills necessary to achieve the organization's mission but the integrity to resolve the value conflicts inherent in shaping the mission.

(Kolb et al., 1986: 13)

The wise leader does not intervene unnecessarily. The leader's presence is felt, but often the group runs itself. . . . Lesser leaders do a lot, say a lot, have followers and form cults. . . . Even worse ones use fear to energize the group and force to overcome resistance. . . . Only the most dreadful leaders have bad reputations.

(Heider, 1986: 33)

The manager is a person with a perpetual preoccupation.

(Mintzberg, 1990: 30)

Managing a counselling agency, the central theme of this book, is, needless to say, a challenging task. Our initial plans for the book were greatly concerned with the details of what and who required managing within counselling services, what detailed policies and systems were required, what methods of financial oversight were implemented and so on. In short, our initial attention was taken up with the mass of detail that requires implementation and monitoring in any organization. Only as the process of writing the later chapters unfolded has our attention been drawn to the vital question of the task of managing as a discrete activity, in and of itself. The recognition that we had not originally conceived this as necessary and important was somewhat of a shock to us. Indeed our preoccupation to attend to the details had somewhat blinded us to the necessity of trying to address the question of what management is.

'Most managers are promoted to management because they are good at something else, something other than management' (Salaman, 1995: 4). This quote somewhat captures our own observations and assumptions about counsellors becoming involved in management roles. Indeed, within the relatively short history of the profession (of counselling/psychotherapy) the management of it as an activity is even shorter. Traditionally, counsellors have worked as independent practitioners or in relatively small organizations, with the exception of national bodies like Relate (formerly the National Marriage Guidance Council). Clearly, these small ventures have required an element of management which has traditionally been supplied by those already in the organization. The explicit role, manager, and the definition of the activity, management, would generally not have been used in the everyday discourse of the practitioners. They would have been doing what was necessary to keep the organization functioning in a more 'organic' rather than structured way. Colleagues would have turned their hand to help where it was required.

More recently, however, with the expansion of the psychotherapy field, many organizations have increased in size and complexity thus requiring the implementation of management structures, systems and indeed personnel. Inevitably, then, in both the voluntary and statutory sectors, 'senior' or experienced counsellors were called on or promoted to assume the management task. A network of university training courses was set up as recently as 1997 to explore the needs of employers of therapists and how these related to both the students' experience during training and the training curricula.

Not only does Salaman (1995) point out that managers are promoted to management because they are good at something else but continues to argue that their earlier skills (as a therapist in our particular case) may actually be an obstacle to the development of management skills! Further, management skills may, in some cases and in some senses, be diametrically opposed to the earlier professional skills and experiences of the counsellor.

A brief case study of one of the authors is pertinent here. After qualifying as a full-time youth worker he was appointed to work initially as a deputy warden in a youth centre. He was one of only two full-time workers there, the other being the warden. There was also a part-time secretary and a small team of part-time youth workers who worked on different evenings. Eighteen months later he was appointed to another centre as warden and was the only full-time worker again having part-time secretarial and youth work assistance. This post obtained for a further three and a half years, after which followed a move to teaching for two years.

Upon completion of counselling training he was employed by a counselling service within a former polytechnic, again one of only two full-timers with a full-time secretary/receptionist. A year later, resourcing was found for a third full-time post and three years after that, the senior colleague retired and he was appointed to that post.

Finally, following a decade of work there, he was appointed to the solitary position of counsellor in a university, with a part-time (afternoons only, term time only) secretary. Ten years later, that service now has three full-time counsellors, has employed up to 12 part-time colleagues in one academic year, a full-time secretary, and has annual vacancies for three trainee counsellors. The size of the present building (reception, store room, seven interviewing rooms, group work room, waiting room, toilets) now limits the activity but the client demands continue to increase.

In this particular scenario, during the early years, the person's capacity to work independently, on their own, for much of the time was much practised. Though his work was for and on behalf of other people (eg. youth club members, the other staff, youth service) for at least half of the time he was the only one in the office. This experience exposed him to the full responsibilities of running an agency with few opportunities for consultation and shared decision making.

The first counselling post was experienced within the confines of a small team, three full-time counsellors and one full-time secretary. The considerable expansion that has occurred within the second counselling service over recent years has enforced the need to appraise critically and assess, again, the very nature of management.

The size of this present organization with its strata of full- and part-time staff, levels of client demand, the different requirements of the employing body and the profession within an overall context of increased expectations of counselling and decreased psychiatric resources has meant that very serious attention indeed has had to be paid to managing rather than clinical work. At the time of writing, this balance of professional activity is under further consideration, where the manager's clinical work is to be reduced even further because of the requirements of the management process.

The demands of fulfilling a much more explicit management role have been considerable and both personally and professionally challenging. Indeed, the writing of this book, though instructive through further reading and considered reflection, leaves this particular co-author slightly embarrassed with his own management shortfalls.

Several critical elements emerge from this scenario that are worth noting here:

■ Most counselling service managers have become so because they were primarily good at something else (eg. reasonably competent at being counsellors).
■ 'Many managers find management difficult' (Salaman, 1995). The multiple tasks and demands of being a manager (some of which are detailed later in this chapter) can prove extremely taxing and exhausting. Perversely, staff perceptions of managers may include little appreciation of the value or complexity of managers' work.
■ Managers of counselling agencies may also be active therapists for some of their time and thus have to balance complex demands (of being a therapist and of being a manager) intrapsychically and practically. Both activities may produce contradictory values and actions.
■ Management can be a lonely task.
■ The demands of the size of the agency intensify the need for more clear and coherent management structures, interventions and general activity.
■ The size of agency and complexity of staffing structures (eg. full-time, part-time, paid, voluntary, professional, secretarial, cleaning) will determine different methods of management intervention, communication, staff dynamics, etc.
■ 'Managers do a large number of different things' (Salaman, 1995). Managing can involve multiple activities exemplified by the notion of a 'way of doing' in direct contrast to many therapeutic approaches that espouse a 'way of being'.

Three areas of management activity can be defined as:

(a)   specialist knowledge and functioning (in this case as a therapist)
(b)   maintenance and development of service in the face of client demands, reduced resources, etc. and
(c)   responsibility for the work of others (Salaman, 1995).

The last point, in contemporary management thinking, can be transposed into the skills of helping colleagues learn and improve, helping them to do what they do better. This is a particularly complex point as it relates to already highly qualified professional colleagues in a counselling agency. Therapists are most often highly dedicated professionals, probably already experienced in a previous profession, who have chosen to now work with individuals in distress. Working with individuals in this way has consciously and deliberately been chosen sometimes against the background of unsatisfactory experiences in other work settings. Though deeply committed to personal learning, development and improvement, both for themselves and their clients, they may not be comfortable with the organizational and management demands of the counselling setting. Indeed the counsellor may not appreciate the activities the manager engages in, in their management role. Mental health professionals may therefore prove to be a very complex group to manage!

The Manager as Oppressor?

From the employees' (counsellors') perspective there can also be a sense of frustration (and this can extend right through to alienation) with the boss. Many counsellors in conversation in supervision and at conferences complain about their managers. Either 'the manager doesn't understand' or 'is imposing draconian measures' or 'is completely out of touch' . . ., etc. Often, the manager can appear (or be projected upon) as insensitive, incompetent, unknowledgeable, interpersonally unskilled, without vision, obstructive, manipulative, power crazy and so on. 'Being a member of the management elite puts one at loggerheads with others . . .' (Zeldin, 1994: 151).

The above dynamics form a regularly recurring phenomenon across a wide range of work settings. What happens when workers (counsellors) become bosses (managers)? Is there something inherent in the management role that sets them up for projection, misunderstanding, oppressive behaviour and so on? Do they fill out, inflated by their own ego, into something that their former professional roles had previously contained or couldn't have imagined?! As Orbach (1997: Foreword) has noted:

> We are confused about leadership. We can't quite decide whether we like it, whether we think it's a good idea, whether we just prefer to knock it. When leaders appear awkward, we take pot shots at them, rather than use the moment to try and understand what we expect, what we want and what we require.

Where to put the Emphasis? Management Issues or Clinical Issues?

The appropriate exercise of role and authority and the manner in which these are achieved within a counselling service are matters of great concern for the aspiring and sitting occupants of management positions. Getting work done with and through others is a central tenet of management work. The manager has to wrestle with such complexities as (a) the 'motivation' and stimulation of staff, (b) the provision of adequate support systems, (c) the sharing of decision making and responsibility giving, (d) resolving inter-staff disputes (e) ensuring equitable treatment across the workforce and so on. Indeed, depending upon the numbers of staff involved, the manager of a counselling service may have to shift their emphasis from being a counsellor with management responsibilities to being a manager whose primary focus is the staff team and only secondarily do some occasional clinical work. Such a change of emphasis in working patterns will hopefully ensure that the staff are sufficiently supported and interacted with to facilitate their own optimum performance. The negative side, however, might mean that the manager's counsellor self is not only not practised regularly but indeed may fall short of sufficient clinical hours to maintain regular professional accredited status.

The Manager as Intermediary

Theodore Zeldin alludes to the role of manager as intermediary (1994). He charts the history of the emergence of the role of the intermediary, recognizing that:

> . . . there used to be a clear division between what the timid and brave could achieve. All the most prized rewards went to those who gave orders while those who did what they were told were more or less despised. But there is a third kind of activity in which the timid and the brave can be on equal terms. Intermediaries can achieve more than their own personal talents permit. (1994: 154)

Zeldin suggests that priests were the first to become intermediaries, winning enormous prestige, negotiating between human frailty and divine strength. Later, merchants became intermediaries but not with the same success. Historically Zeldin suggests that it has taken about 2500 years for intermediaries to become appreciated and that this transformation occurred rather suddenly as a consequence of the new understanding in chemistry that two substances could be combined to form a third. The ideas of catalysis gave intermediaries a new status (1994: 135). The value of intermediaries lies essentially in two important truths. One is that force is no longer in total command. Where intermediaries flourish nobody is oppressed and all parties remain equally pleased. Secondly, being an intermediary means operating essentially at the interpersonal level, the already chosen work arena for counsellors.

Counsellors, by virtue of their training, their theoretical preferences and their philosophies tend towards values such as respect for others, democratic processes, equality of opportunity and a belief in dialogue to resolve disagreements. The counsellor turned manager has thus a broadly similar values base to those of the counsellors in his or her service. A commitment to such shared ideals as offered above hopefully will enhance the efficacy of the counselling manager's job with staff in the agency.

The Impact of Personality on Managing: Enhancing Awareness

Despite recognizing the validity of the above argument, ie. that managers and counselling staff may share certain philosophic values, recognition also has to be taken of the impact of different personalities upon management processes.

Various questionnaires exist that are often used in management training with the purpose of enhancing the awareness of each participant's personal styles of interacting with others. In addition, attendees on management training courses also coincidentally have their awareness raised of other different and equally legitimate styles that may be employed by their colleagues and which, when in direct opposition, can cause very considerable rifts between staff members and the manager.

Three particular examples are offered here. They are: (a) The Myers–Briggs Type Indicator; (b) Belbin Team Roles Self-Perception Inventory; and (c) A communication exercise (in Casse, 1980). Each of these, in their own way, can be used to stimulate reflection on one's personality and interpersonal style thus hopefully creating a heightened awareness of the many different ways people function and communicate in the world.

The Myers–Briggs Type Indicator

The Myers–Briggs Type Indicator was originally designed by Katherine Briggs and Isabel Briggs Myers for specific use in career and development guidance work. It provides a personality measure which gives information on a person's styles and preferences in four broad dimensions of individual differences. These factors are based on Carl Jung's theory of conscious mental functioning and follows his suggestion that each person will have a preference in their information-gathering and decision-making processes towards one pole or the other of each dimension.

These dimensions are:

Extravert	–	Introvert	(EI)
Sensing	–	Intuition	(SN)
Thinking	–	Feeling	(TF)
Judgement	–	Perception	(JP)

The preferences on each dimension are defined as follows: EXTRAVERTS gain their energy from and direct their perception and decision making to the external world of things and other people; INTROVERTS are energized by and direct their attention and decision making to the inner world of ideas and thoughts. SENSING types base their perceptions on the five senses and the immediate evidence of concrete reality; INTUITIVE types base their perceptions on meanings, patterns and associations in the information they pick up. THINKING types arrive at decisions through the impersonal application of rigorous logical principles; FEELING types arrive at decisions on the basis of personal and social values. JUDGING types have a preference for making decisions over taking in information;

PERCEIVING types have a preference for taking in information over making decisions.

The Myers–Briggs questionnaire is composed of (a) some questions seeking the respondent's preferences between two alternatives and (b) some word choices from pairs of 'values'. It can be self-scored by the respondent and then further expansions of the findings may be offered by the questionnaire given and developed by the person concerned.

The 'results' of a Myers–Briggs test therefore offers the person an indicator of their preferred modes of being (as detailed above) with supplementary explanations, and also includes their preferences in perception (sensing, intuitions) and decision making (thinking, feeling).

The Belbin Self-Perception Team Roles Inventory

> For many years, the search for successful management has been seen almost exclusively as a search for the right individual. . . . Any attempts to list the qualities of a good manager demonstrates why this person cannot exist: far too many of the qualities are mutually exclusive. They must be highly forceful and at the same time sensitive to people's feelings. They must be a fluent communicator and a good listener . . . and so on. And if you do find this jewel among managers, this paragon of mutually incompatible characteristics, what will you do when they step under a bus, or go to live abroad. . . . (Jay, 1980)

The above quotation is taken from an article originally published in the *Observer Magazine* on the work of Dr Meredith Belbin and his associates. Belbin's considerable research effort over many years has contributed to our understanding of the successful functioning of teams, a far better and more reliable medium for productivity than the lone manager, however good he or she is.

Belbin's work suggests that the sorts of roles we are likely to adopt in groups remain reasonably consistent across a range of applications. A person's characteristics are likely to be similar whether serving on a community centre management committee or working in an office team to improve the design of a jet engine.

Over a seven-year period Belbin and his colleagues generated a vast amount of data, testing and revising hypotheses, based on the promotion of three rounds of business games each year with each game featuring eight teams. The game itself remained substantially unchanged, thus providing a reliable research base for the outcomes. As the research progressed eight or nine team roles were identified as crucial to the successful outcomes of a group's work.

Through engaging with the Belbin Self-Perception Team Roles Inventory the participant is explicitly given feedback on their efficacy ratings in each of the team roles and has their own awareness raised of the contributory values that different characteristics can contribute to team working. A great danger can lie in appointing a team of all the cleverest and most talented people that can be found. 'Unfortunately, the most disaster prone team is the one that is exclusively composed of very clever people!' (Jay, 1980). The nine team roles are described below. The names are particular to this work and may therefore not be readily understandable without reference to the brief descriptions given here.

Co-ordinator The co-ordinator is the one who presides over the team and co-ordinates its efforts to meet external goals. The co-ordinator is described as mature, confident and trusting. Being a good chairperson they clarify goals and promote decision making.

Shaper Dynamic, outgoing, highly strung. Challenges, pressurizes, finds ways round obstacles. Some have suggested that teams in action may require a 'social leader' and a 'task' leader. The Shaper is thus the 'task' leader and the co-ordinator the 'social' leader. The principal function of a Shaper is to give a shape to the application of the team's efforts. In personality terms they can be full of nervous energy, outgoing and emotional and can be prone to paranoia. Shapers make things happen.

Plant Creative, imaginative, unorthodox. Solves difficult problems. The Plant is the team's source of original ideas, suggestions and proposals. They are much more concerned with major issues and fundamentals than with details which can sometimes be overlooked.

Monitor evaluator Their most valuable skills are in assimilating, interpreting and evaluating large volumes of complex written material, analysing problems and assessing the judgements and contributions of the others. They are sober, strategic, discerning, introverted. They see all options and judge accurately but may be seen to be a dampener on group processes, a 'cold fish' and a critic rather than a creator.

Implementer The implementer is the practical organizer. They are disciplined, reliable, conservative and efficient. They turn ideas into practical actions. They thrive in stable structures and contribute to them constructively.

Resource investigator Being extrovert, enthusiastic, communicative, the resource investigator explores opportunities and develops outside contacts in order to bring ideas, information and developments back to the team. They can often be the most immediately likeable member of the team. Without the stimulus of others they can become demoralized and ineffective yet within the team they can be good improvisers and active under pressure. A tendency also exists to over-relax when the pressure eases.

Team worker The team worker is the most sensitive of the team and the most aware of individuals' needs and worries, perceiving most clearly the emotional undercurrents of the group. They tend to be social, mild and accommodating. They listen well, are socially supportive and avert friction. Though in normal times the value of their individual contributions may not be as immediately visible as most of the other team roles, the effect is very noticeable indeed when they are not there, especially in times of stress and pressure.

Completer–finisher This team role is concerned both with finishing projects on time as well as competent completion of the task. They are therefore painstaking, conscientious, often anxious. They look for errors and omissions and can get impatient with and intolerant towards the more casual, laid-back members of the team.

In the two major sources of information for this section (Jay, 1980; Belbin, 1993) only the latter features a ninth role, that of the specialist.

Specialist Is described as single minded, self-starting and dedicated. They can provide knowledge or technical skills in rare supply. Their contributions, however, are restricted to the narrow front of their specialism.

Belbin's work has now been applied to a range of work settings, where, over time, new staff are selected to fill vacant team roles based on their team functions. 'Team typing' is considered to be of more value in circumstances where the team operates in an area of rapid change (eg. in the workforce, in manufacturing techniques, in different markets, where there is competition pressure and need for quick action and decision making). It is of far less significance in situations of reasonable stability over long periods of time.

A new or recently restructured counselling/psychotherapy service or one that is actively seeking new clientele, eg. an Employee Assistance Programme, might benefit considerably from considering the composition of the working team, ensuring that the various necessary roles for successful team functioning are all available within the attributes and skills of the working members.

Awareness of Communication Types
This is a less well-known exercise in management training than the previous examples yet when used has had a considerable enlightening effect upon participants. Entitled 'Communication Value Orientations: A Self Assessment Exercise' it is based upon the initial answering of a questionnaire where one is invited to choose a preferred statement from a choice of two. Forty pairs of statements are thus considered.

This exercise is detailed in a book entitled *Training for the Cross-Cultural Mind* by Pierre Casse (1980: 125–33), where the full text of the questionnaire, details of how to score the exercise and a full explanation of the implications of the results is provided.

The exercise is based upon four value orientations which, it suggests, can be found in any culture or individual and each orientation has a tremendous impact on the way one communicates. The results reveal the participants' preferred dominant and sub-dominant modes of communication.

Style 1 is influenced by the *action* value orientation. People who are strong on this style like action, doing, achieving, getting things done, improving, solving problems. Style 2 is related to the *process* value orientation. People who are strong on this style like facts, organizing, structuring, setting up strategies, tactics. Style 3 is typical of the *people* value orientations. Individuals who are people orientated like to focus on social processes, interactions, communication, team work, social systems, motivation. Style 4 is characterized by the *idea* value orientation. People with the idea orientation like concepts, theories, exchange of ideas, innovation, creativity, novelty.

Already, the reader will be able to intuit that a manager whose dominant or preferred mode of communication is based on an ideas value orientation might well have difficulties communicating with a staff member concerned with process (facts, organizing, structuring, etc.).

Research on this exercise has revealed that everybody possesses the four value orientations to some degree or other. The questionnaire reveals the dominant or preferred mode of communication. Also, the importance of the value orientation changes according to the situations in which people are involved. The orientations are influenced by personality, culture, past and present experiences. Importantly, people do have the capacity to switch styles though in a crisis there is a tendency to revert to the value orientation one is most used to.

Of particular value to groups in training are the developments of this exercise by inviting groups of participants who share similar value orientations to get together: (a) to discuss the details of their style further, (eg. what do they talk about or focus on when they communicate?); and (b) then to consider some guidelines for how they might communicate with others from the different value orientations.

This brief section on methods of enhancing the awareness of managers has offered three approaches that might be tackled within short training courses. The Myers–Briggs is probably the most well known amongst counsellors and psychotherapists. The value of all three approaches is that they offer reasonably concise criteria against which the participants may compare or locate themselves and by implication, also draw the participants' awareness to the causes of difficulty or breakdown in communication patterns between themselves and colleagues.

The Manager as Parent

Work teams or groups can be considered or understood through the analogy of family groupings. Indeed, group analysts argue that some of a person's previous significant relationships often get played out in the work setting. The manager may therefore be the focus of a very complicated range of unconscious projections from the staff in relation to their internalized parental figures, eg. a demanding or strict father, the dependent mother, the emotionally cold/withdrawn parent, the preoccupied or troubled parent who needs looking after.

Though such projections may seldom be understood as such by the employees, the impact in behavioural terms upon the management relationship may be very considerable. Orbach (1997) puts this succinctly when she writes,

> Almost everyone wants to be quietly recognised for their capabilities and encouraged to express their best. An individual with a history of not being supported may create havoc within a group – or for the leader. The leader may find that he or she is being asked to make up for a deficit in the past. This is not made any easier by the fact that neither the person looking for reassurance nor the leader being asked for it is especially aware that these processes are taking place. Instead, an incomprehensible undercurrent of attack or disappointment that is hard to address may undermine the harmony of the group.

In the particular case scenario of this book, both the manager and the counselling staff are likely to have very sophisticated levels of awareness, interpersonal functioning and analytic thinking by nature of their training, their work and their opportunities for reflection through supervision. The interpersonal dynamics that get played out between a counselling service manager and members of counselling staff are likely therefore to be complex, subtle, difficult to understand and so on.

In Winnicottian terms, the litmus test of a manager's success (when viewed psychologically as a 'parent' figure) is the extent to which they are seen as 'good enough'. The notion of the 'good enough' manager carries with it the possibility of a working ambience that will facilitate a working through of difficult issues, have a forgiving quality, and thus provide a healthy climate.

Quite a wide range of job tasks and qualities are often expected and/or demanded of those in management positions. Some of these are briefly alluded to below.

The Manager as Ambassador
The manager has a responsibility to represent and speak on behalf of the organization in external settings. An ambassadorial role implies a concern for public relations, diplomatic skills, working

outside of traditional office hours, working alone outside the agency, fairly representing the agency and mission, etc.

The Manager as Role Model

When managers are competent in their work they can often act as inspirational role models to younger or newer employees. Such a role carries with it uncomfortable aspects of behaviour that may be projected onto the manager. Mearns (1997: 204) offers a story to exemplify this point.

> I remember a meeting I had with Carl Rogers in his home in late 1972. In that meeting he challenged me on how I had been treating him in recent times. I realized that he was right – I had been challenging him and criticizing him at every opportunity both in private meetings and in groups. I realized and spoke in that meeting about the fact that he had been such an important person in my life through his writing, to the extent that I had re-directed my career and moved to the other side of the world. In a way, to establish my separateness and my value, I had got into a thing where I had to put him down.

The Manager as Enabler

Some counselling managers, by virtue of their previous experience (where that experience may have been as therapists) might work to a very clear model of enabling. This therapeutic model may be extended in the manner they operate with their staff members. For example, there have been many applications of the Person-centred Approach within management circumstances (Rogers, 1978; Suhd, 1995). Also there is a rich resource of psychoanalytic writing on organizational dynamics and functions of leadership (Morgan, 1986). The manager as enabler may provide aspects of the organizational consultant's role, trying to facilitate the staff members' reflections on, responsibilities for and contribution to the work.

Related strongly to this positivistic intention is the manager's capacity to handle criticism. Though it will be crucially important to be able to withstand and endure the criticism the successful manager must also be able to 'distil the essence of it so that it can be examined and responded to. . . . Those who do find a way to absorb it, to feel the hurt that can go along with an unprovoked attack and then recover from it, are far more likely to be able to give the kind of leadership that recognizes the strengths and needs of their group (Orbach, 1997).

The Manager as 'Director'

Some managers may exercise their authority in very clear ways through the issuing of requests, demands, preferences, instructions and so on. They may set very clear boundaries for what is and is not required in the particular setting in which they are working. In this case the manager may be very directive.

The Manager as Trouble-shooter and Mediator

> When we do not understand another person who shapes our work and our reality, we are judgemental: we find fault . . . we blame them. (Hirschorn, 1988: 202)

Quite often the manager can find themselves at the centre of a complex tussle occurring between different members of the agency or indeed be the focus of opposition from one or a group of staff. Handy (1976: 212) notes that 'it is perhaps belabouring the obvious but the resolution of differences or potential differences takes up the largest single chunk of managerial time and everything is not always well done at the end of it all'.

The manager's task can be a thankless one in circumstances where there is internal strife within the staff group. Maintaining a balanced and open view of the contentious issue during the disagreement and the effect that it has upon the sub-groups actively disagreeing can sorely tax the most patient of managers.

The Manager as . . . Further Dynamic Issues Affecting the Management Process

> Whenever you advise a ruler in the way of Tao, counsel him not to use force to conquer the universe.
> For this would only cause resistance.
> Thorn bushes spring up whenever the army has passed.
> Lean years follow in the wake of a great war.
> Just do what needs to be done.
> Never take advantage of power. (Heider, 1986: 30)

The series of very brief sections detailed above could, of course, be extended in many directions to encompass a wide range of roles, attributes, skills and knowledge attributable to the management task. The variety of ways, approaches and methods in which managers conduct their work is very broad. Inevitably this breadth will be determined by their personality, culture, gender, previous personal work experiences, self-image, levels of self-esteem, strengths and weaknesses and so on. Additional factors will include their own sense of purpose and perception of their role and its demands and needs. All of these dimensions and more residing within the persona of the manager will have differential effects at different times upon the manager's behaviour and performance in the work setting.

Power Relations

A consideration of the sheer human complexity of the work environment (and the manager's role within that) proves to be an extremely daunting task. However the organization is structured, the relations of power between managers and their staff, their clients, their management committee, and the served community will be constantly present, constituting a continuing dynamic in the overall functioning of the organization. The particular quote used above inevitably carries a strong value base that originates in Taoist thought. From this perspective, a manager might view their role as one of enabling the natural processes of the work environment to unfold. The exercise of power in this example is configurated as a way of acceptant being and supporting of the various initiatives that the service and its staff are engaged in.

This somewhat philosophically orientated stance stands in direct contrast to the rather more 'macho' models of power seeking and Machiavellian endeavour featured in many Hollywood films and contemporary novels. Power inevitably has to be exercised at different times and in different ways relative to the needs of the particular situation, the persons involved and the manager's disposition.

The manager is not simply the potential imposer of power. He or she also resides within a configuration of power systems that impact and impose upon them from many angles. When subordinate members of staff feel that not only are they powerless but that managers are all powerful, they fail to recognize the potential power they have to influence situations. They also fail to recognize that the managers themselves are trying to balance the variety of demands placed upon them from above, outside and within the organization.

In human service organizations, particularly those we are considering here (ie. counselling and psychotherapy agencies) a model of management underpinned by a clear ethical framework, particularly as that relates to the dissemination of power, is a pre-requisite for the continuing honourable delivery of that therapeutic service.

Organizational Values

> To say that in human service organizations questions concerning tasks, priorities, objectives, etc. are constantly contested is to say no more than that within such organizations questions of value are primary. (Hoggett, 1996)

Hoggett's review suggests that the values that underpin the work of counselling agencies are critical to the life and work of that organization. Too often, he asserts, the dominant definition of what a particular organization is all about is a definition which is the outcome of particular relations of power. However, within organizations, there can be a multitude of attributed or perceived aims by the professional staff, the service users, commissioning and referring agents, the ancillary staff, etc. This variety of values is an expression of the connectedness of the organization to society and any notion of 'a primary task', suggests Hoggett, is not only simplistic but potentially destructive.

The multiplicity of meanings attributed by staff to the organization's work runs parallel not only to general post-modernist thinking but also to psychotherapeutic theory where the uniqueness and idiosyncratic nature of each human being is valued and taken as a given in the therapeutic work. Managers are uniquely situated in the organizational structure to appreciate this multiplicity of value attributions made by staff members. The danger of asserting a particular primary task as the task the organization must perform if it is to survive courts the danger of blurring the distinction, crucial to human service organizations, between survival and development (Armstrong, 1996, in Hoggett, 1996).

Hoggett continues this theme in noting that 'when an organization's capacity for development is at risk what we mean is that its capacity to exist as a place with value is now in doubt. We speak, more perceptively than we know, of workers becoming demoralized, ie. of losing a sense of value'.

The general movement for many welfare organizations during recent times has been this very abandonment of development for survival. Consequently staff experience strong feelings that their organization no longer stands for the values and principles which originally attracted them to it. Survival in this sense has come to mean living without value.

We can see here, using the above analysis that the manager's care-taking task of the overall organization, particularly in stringent political and economic times is very considerable indeed.

Hoggett extends his hypothesis mentioned above to the distinction between task and purpose. 'As I see it', he suggests, 'the concept of purpose is one saturated with value, ie. with a sense of what is good and bad, right and wrong, for me/my organization to be doing'. His argument is that if a group or organization is to provide a facilitating environment for development to occur (a crucial aim of counselling agencies) it must have a sense of purpose. This sense is necessarily ambiguous, thus enabling agreement to be reached and at the same time facilitating each staff member's capacity to infuse the work with personal meaning. Such temporary definitions of purpose are therefore fictions which serve to bind the group together and contain differences without crushing them.

Hoggett constructs the inner confidence gained by organizations from such a position with what he calls 'lapel-badge' approaches to values. These are exemplified by the recent fashion in mission statements, chartermarks, Investors In People awards and so on. At worst this is a check-list approach which reduces values and purpose to elements of strategy, useful only in establishing where the organization is in the pecking order of the market place. Beyond that, they can have the effect of moving the workers' own sense of personal meaning they bring to the work to a reduced and externalized set of statements of criteria. Personal responsibility, vision, commitment and worthwhileness are just some of the personal values in danger of being lost and abandoned by the various staff members in such a climate. Therapists, like many others in the helping professions, are generally highly motivated, self-directing, responsible people. Such traits and aspirations are absolutely necessary to their psychologically healthy functioning as mental health workers.

The above analysis of recent trends in human service organizations points, yet again, to the crucial and indeed pivotal role of the manager who works at the intersection of the organization with society, that point of contact (some might say ferment) between the inner and the outer, the professional aspirations of therapy and the contemporary social demands of the immediate environment. The temptations to wrap the present (in this case the delivery of ethically sound and professionally competent therapy) in very shiny and eye-catching plastic wrapping (mission statements, quality standards, published lists of procedures, etc.) that actually may have little essence or meaning for the staff are very high indeed. The manager, desperate for enhanced resourcing of an underfunded service will be under considerable pressure to demonstrate, in as many ways as possible, how valuable and worthwhile the work of the agency is. The loneliness, subtleties and dangers of their position are starkly exemplified in the above situation. Driven by demands of the outer societal context, the manager feels forced to present the best evidence and image of the agency. Concerned, at the same time, to care sensitively and competently for the ideals of the work and the colleagues employed to do that work, s/he must maintain an optimum communication flow and openness to many points of view.

The balancing of these potent and sometimes contradictory pressures is a constituent part of the manager's lot. It goes without saying that our own view is that managers (as well as therapists) require professional support and consultancy to combat the stresses, strains and potential isolation of their roles. The public sphere in which management work is carried out is in direct contrast to the private arena of therapy. Managing therapy and therapists, therefore, presents complicated challenges.

Dimensions of Management that are Rarely Considered

In a diagram using the above title, Walton (1997: 108) encourages workplace counsellors to appreciate the complex nature of management and how their clients (the employees) are affected perceptually and behaviourally by the organization's culture. From the perspectives of the counselling service manager (the focus of this book) these dimensions will be of particular interest and concern in the maintenance of staff morale, support and competent clinical performance. These rarely considered dimensions include the management relationship to and of:

- ambiguity
- collective anxiety and insecurity
- meanings
- dilemmas

- ethics
- issues other than rational factors
- continuity
- conflicting priorities
- people's relatedness.

The shadow side of management/staff relations generally referred to in the above list (and more specifically in the phrase, 'issues other than rational factors'), can prove an extremely complicated and indeed distressing element for the manager to deal with. This arena of concern has already been acknowledged in the previous section's 'manager as parent' and 'manager as trouble-shooter' and is returned to again in the next section. This whole subject is dealt with substantively in the edited book *The Unconscious at Work* (Obholzer and Zagia Roberts, 1994).

The Size of the Agency – Managers and Sub-managers

The opening sentences to this section are in great danger of so stating the obvious that they may appear crass, oversimplistic and indeed banal! Their essence unfolds something like this: the larger the agency, the more complex are the resulting group dynamics and inner tensions experienced by the staff group. Complexity in this sense is construed as relative to the critical size of the agency.

An independent practice featuring three or four colleagues who work in a co-operative way, employing a part-time cleaner and receptionist/secretary is at the other end of the spectrum from the counselling agency that offers a national service through sub-contracted employees. Somewhere between these two extremes lie agencies that may variously 'employ' anything from eight to 30 or 40 counsellors. The term 'employ' in the previous sentence is deliberately set in quotes in order to clarify that this engagement may be full-time, part-time, paid, unpaid, regular, infrequent and so on. A wide variety of counselling services are very familiar with having such a cross section of staff, not only for the therapists but also the ancillary roles of administration, reception, finance, cleaning, etc.

The manager is thus critically positioned somewhere within a vortex of staff communication dynamics, expectations, political aspirations and unconscious projections even in circumstances where the organization is so big and/or dispersed that levels of personal contact between manager and colleagues is minimal or non-existent.

Within analytic group work perspectives, the dynamics of small groups have been likened to family processes and those of larger groups as analogous to society. Whatever the size of the organization, the manager has to seriously consider how best might the needs of the agency be served. Unlike national industries, where, for example, all staff may be employed on full-time salaries in regional area office units each having their own local manager, some counselling organizations may have individual counsellors operating in different cities. The task of management, at a distance, of such 'contracted' personnel may prove most problematic.

Social interaction patterns in large groups (parallel to society) are complex, multifaceted, lack singular or linear meaning and indeed may be contradictory and thus defy simple understanding. The principal manager of large counselling organizations thus has to consider seriously the implementation of a structure of complementary or supplementary management posts and procedures throughout the organization to optimize the potential for delivery of caring, competent professional service to individuals in distress. One of the core aims, then, of such services is to offer quality time and a quality therapeutic relationship to clients. In tandem with this optimum service delivery the manager must strive to do all that is possible to protect and develop the personnel, administrative and financial systems of the organization that support this core therapeutic activity.

Doing Emotional Work

Counselling organizations do emotional work for and on behalf of society. Examples of this include student counselling services which have been described as symbolic containers of colleges' anxieties (Lago and Shipton, 1994). Relate has always been an agency whose work lies at the heart of interpersonal and family life in the UK. Particular Employee Assistance Programmes specialize in supporting stressed or traumatized employees of organizations. In performing this emotional work, therapeutic agencies contribute enormously to the life blood and general quality of life in society.

'Doing emotional work' could be judged to be an inappropriate operationalized phrase emanating from industrial applications, parallel somewhat to producing motor cars or selling merchandise! Taking this analysis for the moment, however, the work in this sense is often:

- time allocated (50 minute therapeutic sessions)
- time restricted (short-term contracts)
- multi-productive (counsellors may see five or six clients each day)
- governed by performance and quality standard criteria (evaluation outcomes)
- overlaid by standards of production (ethical codes, supervision, complaints procedures)
- costed (client fees) and possibly
- profit making.

In this stark, reductionist, mechanistic analysis the therapist acts as a particular sort of technician whose task is to get the client 'up and running' again. The manager, in turn, acts in a whole variety of ways to optimize the delivery of the work.

Unlike industrial applications of work, however, doing emotional work has emotional implications for all those involved. This statement does not deny that work itself is an emotional environment for all employees. Rather it is important to acknowledge that human beings who work as therapists also need to have their own emotional lives tended to and nurtured. This need, of course, has been professionally recognized over many years and consequently processes such as personal therapy, consultancy and supervision have not only emerged but have been deemed to be critical elements in therapist training and practice (Dryden, 1995; Proctor, 1997). The impact of working as a counsellor/therapist has been discussed in Chapter 6 under Burnout and Vicarious Traumatization.

In short, managers must ensure good working conditions for their counselling staff that recognize the enormous emotional impact the work can have on each practitioner. Mechanisms for internal support, mentoring, supervision (internal and external) will all have to be considered and then implemented. (Proctor [1997] offers useful contributions on the distinctions between management practice, internal and external supervision.)

The above resources are thus well established at the level of individual practitioners. Less well developed, however, are the supportive mechanisms available to managers responsible for therapeutic organizations. 'Even with the most sensitive leadership styles, the leader faces potential isolation' (Orbach, 1997). Managers' support groups, management mentoring and coaching schemes and individual consultancy may all be very good ways of supporting and enhancing each manager's work.

Critically, managers must also be sensitive to the very serious demands put on their agencies by that immediate part of society they are serving and recognize the uncomfortable reality that their own agency is somewhat of a microcosm or reflection of that wider picture.

A manager must ensure, therefore, that systems are in place:

(a) to maintain the health and efficacy of the individual therapists employed (eg. supervision)
(b) to maintain their own health and optimum performance levels (eg. management training, support mechanisms)
(c) to support non-counselling colleagues within the organization who are inevitably exposed to the consequences of this emotional work and finally
(d) to recognize, monitor and openly discuss, on an organizational basis, the full implications of being an organization doing emotional work. Various public responsibilities or tasks may emerge from this fourth aspect that involve the appropriate communication of issues arising in the therapeutic work to a wider audience. This 'mirroring' function, which must be ethically boundaried, well evidenced and sensitively transmitted and which can be very valuable to those responsible for decision making in the wider context is manifestly a management responsibility. The manager has to be rigorous in their data interpretation, conscientiously committed and sensitive in their public transmission of this knowledge.

This further 'intertwining' element of the inner private, discrete work of the therapists with the political, cultural and social transmission of the (appropriate) knowledge derived from such work to a wider arena reminds us yet again of the particular tight rope the successful manager must negotiate in fulfilling the extensive demands of their work.

Concluding Thoughts

This chapter has ranged across a wide spectrum of the inter-personal implications of the manager's role. Such phenomena as role ambiguity and flexibility are both implicit and explicit in what has been written. What does the manager do in specific circumstances? Who knows whether these actions are right or wrong? What impact do the implications of their behaviour have upon the staff team?

'Morale and productivity do not necessarily go together' asserts Charles Handy (1976: 97). Harmony may therefore be affected by a manager's behaviour but quantity and quality of work carried out by the staff may not be affected similarly. The reverse is also true.

A manager's style and behaviour, of course, not only will variously impact upon each individual staff member, but will be ameliorated or exaggerated through what else is happening or has happened in their own lives. The impact of the manager will also be experienced by the group of staff and this 'group sensing' or evaluation of the manager's performance could be different again to both what the manager intends in their behaviour and to what each individual staff member experiences. A complex role indeed! '[M]anagement, like politics, consists to a large degree in the management of differences . . . groups and individuals in organizations have different roles/goals/skills/tasks . . . the blending of these differences into one coherent whole is the overall task of management' (Handy, 1976: 122).

Appendix

A University Counselling Service – Complaints Procedure

1. The professionalism of the department and its commitment to providing a quality service to clients and the University make it important that it has a clear, equitable and speedy procedure for investigating and responding to complaints.
2. As a point of principle it is important that every effort is made to resolve the complaint at an informal level initially. At this point it will be made clear to the person making the complaint that there is a formal process and they have a right to use it.
3. On receipt of a formal complaint related to the work of the Service, an internal inquiry will be set in motion to investigate the complaint as a matter of urgency. The complainant will be informed by letter that this procedure has commenced.
4. The complaint will be investigated by a panel of two counsellors who are not involved directly in the situation giving rise to the complaint; one of the panel will be the Head of the Counselling Service (who will convene the panel) except when the Head of the Service is the subject of the complaint, when one of the Senior Counsellors will convene the panel. The panel will also include an independent counsellor to ensure a view from outside the Service is available.
5. The panel will request a written response to the complaint from the counsellor concerned, and will meet to consider the substance of the complaint and the counsellor's response. At this meeting, the panel may decide that it has sufficient evidence to resolve the matter. If not, it may take one or both of the following steps:
   5.1 Invite the counsellor concerned to meet the panel and consider further the circumstances underlying the case.
   5.2 Invite the complainant to meet the panel to clarify the complaint further, at which meeting the complainant may be accompanied by a friend.

6. Once the panel feel they have sufficient information available to come to a conclusion, they shall summarize their findings in writing. The summary will include:

    6.1 A résumé of the circumstances giving rise to the complaint.

    6.2 A résumé of the counsellor's response

    6.3 An indication of any outstanding dispute over matters of fact.

    6.4 A recommendation of any further action to be expected of the Service regarding the particular case.

    6.5 A recommendation for any changes in Service policy or practice to avoid future occurrences.

    6.6 A recommendation about whether the issues involved in the case need to be drawn to the attention of the senior management of the University.

7. The Head of the Counselling Service (or a Senior Counsellor acting as deputy) shall communicate by letter to the complainant the outcome of the internal inquiry, and will remind the complainant that, if not satisfied with this response, he/she may take the issue further by complaining to the Registrar and Secretary of the University.

8. Implications arising from the inquiry will be considered at the next business meeting of the counselling team.

9. If the internal inquiry finds a prima facie case that a counsellor has acted in an unprofessional manner, or has breached BAC Code of Ethics and Practice, this would then become a matter for disciplinary proceedings within the University and for referral to the Standards and Ethics Committee of BAC.

10. It is of utmost importance that the following good practices shall be adopted throughout the consideration of the complaint:

    10.1 All meetings to consider the complaint to be carefully minuted; any subsequent telephone calls from the complainant to be noted, with a request for confirmation in writing of the further points being made.

    10.2 Consideration of the complaint to be treated as a matter of priority - for example, the acknowledgement letter to the complainant to be sent out within five working days of receipt of the complaint and to arrange any further meetings within a few days.

11. This complaints procedure shall be reviewed annually by the Counselling Service.

March 1995

Bibliography

ACAS (1988) *Employee Appraisal*, Advisory Booklet No. 2. London: HMSO.

Albee, G.W. (1977) 'The Protestant Ethic, Sex and Psychotherapy', *American Psychologist*, 32: 150–61.

American Psychiatric Association (1994) *Diagnostic and Statistical Manual of Mental Disorders*, 4th edn (*DSM-IV*). Washington DC: American Psychiatric Association.

Appleyard, B. (1993) *Understanding the Present: Science and the Soul of Modern Man*. London: Picador.

Armstrong, D. (1996) 'The Recovery of Meaning'. Paper presented to the IPSO Annual Symposium *Organisation 2,000: Psychoanalytic Perspectives*. (June), New York.

BAC Code of Ethics (1993) Invitation to Membership. Rugby: British Association for Counselling.

BAC Information Sheet No. 12: *Setting up a Counselling Service*. Rugby: British Association for Counselling.

Bank, J. (1992) *The Essence of Total Quality Management*. London: Prentice Hall.

Belbin, M. (1993) *Team Roles at Work*. Oxford: Butterworth-Heinemann.

Benacly, A. (1995) 'Making It Plain'. *The Guardian* (Society section). 18 October: 2.

Bond, T. (1996) 'Counselling-Supervision', in S. Palmer, S. Dainow and P. Milner (eds), *Counselling: The BAC Counselling Reader*. London: Sage.

Brandon, D. (nd) 'Zen and the Art of Interviewing', unpublished essay.

Breakwell, G.M. (1989) *Facing Physical Violence*. London: BPS Books and Routledge.

Burrows, R. (1995) 'Issues around Setting up a Counselling Service', *Counselling*, 6 (2): 121–3.

Carroll, J.F.X. and White, W.L. (1982) 'Theory Building: Integrating Individual and Environmental Factors within an Ecological Framework', in W.S. Paurie (ed.), *Job Stress and Burnout: Research, Theory and Intervention Perspectives*. Beverly Hills, CA: Sage.

Carroll, M. and Walton, M. (1997) *Handbook of Counselling in Organisations*. London: Sage.

Carsley, C. (1995) 'Taking the Plunge: A Psychodynamic Counsellor's Experience of Beginning in Private Practice', *Counselling*, 6 (2): 124–6.

Cascio, W.F. (1995) *Managing Human Resources: Productivity, Quality of Work Life, Profits*. Maidenhead: McGraw-Hill.

Casse, P. (1980) *Training for the Cross-Cultural Mind*. Washington DC: Society for Intercultural Education Training and Research.

Clarkson, P. (1995) *The Therapeutic Relationship*. London: Whurr.

Concise Oxford Dictionary (1974). London: Oxford University Press.

Conradi, P. (1995) Extract from an interview with Colin Lago in preparation of this book.

Crouan, M. (1994) 'The Contribution of a Research Study Toward Improving a Counselling Service', *Counselling*, 5 (1) (February): 32–4.

Culley, S. and Wright, J. (1997) 'Brief and Time Limited Counselling, in S. Palmer and G. McMahon (eds), *Handbook of Counselling* (2nd edn). London: Routledge. pp. 252–65.

Daines, B., Gask, L. and Usherwood, T. (1997) *Medical and Psychiatric Issues for Counsellors*. London: Sage.

Draucker, C.B. (1992) *Counselling Survivors of Childhood Sexual Abuse*. London: Sage.

Dryden, W. (1995) *The Stresses of Counselling in Action*. London: Sage.

Ellenberger, H.F. (1970) *The Discovery of the Unconscious: The History and Evaluation of Dynamic Psychiatry*. London: Allen Lane.

Embleton Tudor, L. and Tudor, K. (1995) 'Temenos – The Creation and Integration of Therapeutic Space', unpublished manuscript (available from the authors at Temenos, 13 Penrhyn Road, Sheffield S11 8UL).

Feng, G-F. and English, J. (1972) *Lao Tsu: Tao Te Ching*. Aldershot, Hants.: Wildwood House.

Fletcher, C. (1994) 'Performance Appraisal in Context: Organisational Changes and their Impact on Practice', in N. Anderson and P. Herriot (eds), *Assessment and Selection in Organisations: Methods and Practice for Recruitment and Appraisal*. Chichester: John Wiley & Sons.

Flew, A. (1972) *An Introduction to Western Philosophy: Ideas and Argument from Plato to Sartre*. London: Croom Helm.

Gabriel, M.A. (1994) 'Group Therapists and Aids Groups: an Exploration of Traumatic Stress Reactions', *Group*, 18 (3): 167–76.

Gray, A. (1994) *An Introduction to Therapeutic Frame*. London: Routledge.

The Group at the Francis Centre, Derby (1984) 'Turning Points in Establishing the Centre', *Counselling*, 49 (August).

Hall, E.T. (1969) *The Hidden Dimension*. New York: Anchor Books/Doubleday.

Hall, E.T. (1983) *The Dance of Life: The Other Dimension of Time*. New York: Anchor Books/Doubleday.

Handy, C.B. (1976) *Understanding Organisations*. Harmondsworth: Penguin.

Hasenfeld, Y. (1992) *The Nature of Human Service Organisations*. London: Sage.

Hasenfeld, Y. and Schmid, H. (1989) 'The Life Cycle of Human Service Organisations', *Administration in Social Work*, (13): 243–69.

Haynes, J. and Wiener, J. (1996) 'The Analyst in the Counting House: Money as Symbol and Reality in Analysis', *British Journal of Psychotherapy*, 13 (1): 14-25.

Heider, J. (1986) *The Tao of Leadership*. London: Wildwood House.

Herriot, P. (1987) 'The Selection Interview', in P. Warr (ed.), *Psychology at Work*, 3rd edn. Harmondsworth: Penguin. Ch. 7.

Hirschorn, L. (1988) *The Workplace Within: Psychodynamics of Organisational Life*. Cambridge, MA: MIT Press.

Hoggett, P. (1996) *Review of* 'The Unconscious at Work: Individual and Organisational Stress in the Human Services'. A. Obholzer and V. Zagia Roberts (eds), London: Routledge 1994 in Free Associations accessible on http://www.shef.ac.uk/2/psysc/rmy/hogg.htm/.

Holmes, J. and Lindley, R. (1991) *The Values of Psychotherapy*. Oxford: Oxford University Press.

Howe, D. (1993) *On Being A Client: Understanding the The Process of Counselling & Psychotherapy*. London: Sage.

Jacobs, M. (1981) 'Setting the Record Straight', *Counselling*, 36 (April): 10-15.

James, J., Howell, J. and Rosillo, E. (1985) 'The Nottingham Counselling Centre', *Counselling*, 54 (November): 9-15.

Jay, A. (1980) 'Nobody's Perfect but a Team Can Be', *Observer Magazine*, 20 April.

Jenkins, P. (1996) 'Counselling and the Law', in S. Palmer, S. Dainow and P. Milner (eds), *The BAC Counselling Reader*. London: Sage.

Jenkins, P. (1997) *Counselling, Psychotherapy and the Law*. London: Sage.

Katz, A. (1995) 'The Keys are on the Couch', *The Guardian* (Society), 29: 7.

Kolb, D., Lublin, S., Spoth, J and Baker, R. (1986) 'Strategic Management Development', *Journal of Management Development*, 5 (3): 13-24.

Lago, C.O. (1981) 'Establishing a Counselling Centre: A Survey of Counselling Projects in their Early Days', *Counselling*, 36 (April): 18-25.

Lago, C.O. (1996) 'Computer Therapeutics', *Counselling*, 7 (4): 287-9.

Lago, C.O. (1997) 'Counselling and the Internet', *Fedora* (European Counselling and Guidance Association) (Oct): 15-17.

Lago, C.O. and Shipton, G.A. (1994) *On Listening and Learning: Student Counselling in Further and Higher Education*. London: Central Book Publishing.

Lago, C.O. and Thompson, J. (1996) *Race, Culture and Counselling*. Buckingham: Open University Press.

Lewis, J., Clark, D. and Morgan, D. (1992) *Whom God Hath Joined Together: The History of Marriage Guidance*. London: Routledge.

McCall, J. (1996) *Statistics: A Guide for Therapists*. Oxford: Butterworth-Heinemann.

McCann, L. and Pearlman, A. (1990) 'Vicarious Traumatization: A Framework for Understanding the Psychological Effects of Working with Victims', *Journal of Traumatic Stress*, 3 (1).

McLeod, J. (1993) *An Introduction to Counselling*. Buckingham: Open University.

McLeod, J. (1994a) 'The Research Agenda for Counselling', *Counselling*, 5 (1): 41-3.

McLeod, J. (1994b) 'Issues in the Organisation of Counselling: Learning from NMGC', *British Journal of Guidance and Counselling*, 22 (2): 163-74.

Mearns, D. (1997) *Person Centred Counselling Training*. London: Sage.

Meichenbaum, D. (1997) *Treating Post Traumatic Stress Disorder: A Handbook and Practice Manual for Therapy*. Chichester: John Wiley & Sons.

Mintzberg, H. (1990) 'The Manager's Job: Folklore and Fact', *Harvard Business Review*, (March/April): 163-76.

Morgan, G. (1986) *Images of Organization*. Beverly Hills, CA: Sage.

Morgan, G. (1989) (ed.) *Creative Organization Theory: A Resource Book*. London: Sage.

Muchinsky, P.M. (1986) 'Personnel Selection Methods' in C.L. Cooper and I. Robertson (eds), *International Review of Industrial and Organisational Psychology*. Chichester: John Wiley & Sons.

North Derbyshire and South Derbyshire Health (1995) *Guidelines for the Employment of Counsellors in General Practice*.

Obholzer, A. and Zagia Roberts, V. (eds) (1994) *The Unconscious at Work: Individual and Organizational Stress in the Human Services*. London: Routledge.

Oldfield, S. (1983) *The Counselling Relationship: A Study of the Clients' Experience*. London: Routledge & Kegan Paul.

O'Leary, E. (1992) *Gestalt Therapy: Theory, Practice and Research*. London: Chapman & Hall.

Orbach, S. (1997) 'Leading Questions', *The Guardian* (Weekend). 6 December.

Palmer, S. and McMahon, G. (eds) (1997) *Client Assessment*. London: Sage.

Penguin Dictionary of Modern Quotations (1976). Harmondsworth: Penguin.

Proctor, B. (1997) 'Supervision for Counsellors in Organizations', in M. Carroll and M. Walton (eds), *Handbook of Counselling in Organizations*, London: Sage.

Randall, G. (1994) 'Employee Appraisal', in K. Sisson (ed.), *Personnel Management: A Comprehensive Guide to Theory and Practice in Britain*. Oxford: Blackwell.

Ratigan, B. (1981) 'Leicester Counselling Centre Project: Accreditation, Supervision, Training', *Counselling*, 36 (April): 5-9.

Rogers, C.R. (1978) *Carl Rogers on Personal Power: Inner Strength and its Revolutionary Impact*. London: Constable.

Roget's Thesaurus (1972). Harmondsworth: Penguin.

Rosenfield, M. (1997) *Counselling by Telephone*. London: Sage.

Ross, P. (1996) 'Counselling and Accountability', in S. Palmer, S. Dainow and P. Milner (eds), *Counselling: The BAC Counselling Reader*. London: Sage.

Ruddell, P. (1997) 'General Assessment Issues' in S. Palmer and G. McMahon (eds), *Client Assessment*. London: Sage.

Salaman, G. (1995) *Managing*. Buckingham: Open University Press.

Sanders, P. (1993) *An Incomplete Guide to Using Counselling Skills on the Telephone*. Manchester: PCSS Books.

Scott, M.J. and Stradling, S.G. (1992) *Counselling for Post-Traumatic Stress Disorder*. London: Sage.

Scull, A. (1975) 'From madness to mental illness: medical men as moral entrepreneurs', *European Journal of Sociology*, 16: 281-61.

Scull, A. (1979) *Museums of Madness: The Social Organisations of Insanity in Nineteenth Century England*. London: Allen Lane.

Sheffield University Counselling Service (1997) 'What to do if a Counsellor is not Immediately Available', information leaflet (2nd edn).

Sherwood Psychotherapy Training Institute Ltd (1996) *Code of Ethics and Professional Practice*. Sherwood Psychotherapy Training Institute: Nottingham.

Shirom, A. (1989) 'Burnout in Work Organisations', in C.L. Cooper and I.T. Robertson (eds), *International Review of Industrial and Organisational Psychology*. Chichester: John Wiley & Sons. Ch. 2.

Sills, C. (ed.) (1997) *Contracts in Counselling*. London: Sage.

Smith, D. (1991) *Hidden Conversations: An Introduction to Communicative Psychoanalysis*. London: Routledge.

Straker, G. and Moosa, F. (1994) 'Interacting with Trauma Survivors in Contexts of Continuing Trauma', *Journal of Traumatic Stress*, 7 (3): 457-65.

Suhd, M. (1995) *Positive Regard: Carl Rogers and Other Notables he Influenced*. Palo Alto, CA: Science and Behaviour Books.

Telephone Helplines Group (1993) *Telephone Helplines: Guidelines for Good Practice*. London: Broadcasting Support Services.

Traynor, B. and Clarkson, P. (1996) 'What Happens if a Psychotherapist Dies?', in S. Palmer, S. Dainow and P. Milner (eds), *Counselling: The BAC Counselling Reader*. London: Sage.

Tudor, K. (1997) 'Social Contracts: Contracting for Social Change' in C. Sills (ed.) *Contracts in Counselling*. London: Sage.

Wallis, J.H. and Booker, H.S. (1958) *Marriage Counselling*. London: Routledge & Kegan Paul.

Walton, M. (1997) 'Organization Culture and its Impact on Counselling', in M. Carroll and M. Walton (eds), *Handbook of Counselling in Organizations*. London: Sage.

Wood, J.K. (1990) 'Everything and Nothing: Client-Centred Therapy, The Person-Centred Approach and Beyond'. Brazil. Privately published document.

Yontef, G. (1993) *Awareness Dialogue and Process: Essays on Gestalt Therapy*. New York: Gestalt Journal Press.

Young, R. (1998) *The UK Internet Starter Kit*. London: Prentice Hall.

Zeldin, T. (1994) *An Intimate History of Humanity*. London: Minerva.

Index